iExperienceKorea

Jeff Rogers

DEDICATION

The book is dedicated to my wife, whose patient support was indispensible to the completion of the manuscript.

CONTENTS

ACKNOWLEDGMENTS

I have to thank my many Korean friends, even the ones who gave me a headache, and especially the ones who I irritated over the years. And of course, I certainly would have gotten nowhere without my beautiful and supportive wife, Myung.

WHAT IS THE IMPACT OF GLOBALIZATION ON CULTURE IN DEVELOPING CULTURES?

There are shadows of confliction at the root of this question in that culture is an isolationist phenomenon whereas globalization is not. Culture differences arise because of isolation in a similar way that DNA differentiation does. Also similar is the way that genetic differentiation begins to disappear when cross-breeding occurs, so likewise cultural differences begin to dissipate when cultures meet and mix.

Interestingly however, the dominant culture in the mix is not normally as obviously, quickly, or agreeably (in a welcoming sense) influenced as is the subordinate culture in the exchange. So in times when American cultural trend have been favored and dominant, it could work rapid and radical changes to a subordinate culture while the culture of the subordinate worked little or no change upon the dominant one.

I don't really see an problem with cultural homogenization in principle, but it can wreak havoc in an effected society if changes happen too fast, destructively severing people from their stabilizing roots. An obvious example of that might be the generation gap between an old-world and pastorally minded grandfather and his upwardly mobile, individualist, self centered, metro sexual grandkids. What I mean is this:

In the west as a dominant culture that seeks its own organic, culturally introspective and naval gazing center, there is gradual change that arises from inside, inclusive of the past incremental generation so there are not really many radical disconnects from one generation to another. But in lands where powerful cultural influences are imported from attention focused outward on other lands, the previous generations are simply left at sea as to what is going on and how to relate to it.

Thus, the tenants of conservatism can work to protect societies if they are strong enough to inhibit cultural destabilization, but they tend to exacerbate the problem and cause certain fractures if they are (1) so weak as to allow culture drift among the young, but yet (2) strong enough to engender stubborn change rejection among the middle aged. And all traditional cultures trend ultra-conservative in nature.

The generational gap is only one aspect of destabilization inherent in rapid cultural change. Morality, ethics, art, metaphysics, social institutions, mental health, diet, physical health, infrastructure, etc.. etc... can all be rapidly destabilized if quickly rebuilt on imported, unfamiliar, inorganic cultural foundations.

Overall however, in a world whose tone is set by multiculturalism, it is not really much of an option to shut one's self or one's society off from some form of global integration. And in a world of more and more rapidly changing progressivism, anti-conformity may even be suicidal for a culture that digs in its heels so resistively so as to prevent successful economic and technical benefits to flow across their border.

What this means is that whether by choice or by osmosis, old cultures are doomed by some degree to fade and one global culture may inexorably impose itself more and more upon the seething masses in the brother hood of man.

ARE KOREANS POSSESSIVE ABOUT K-POP?

Koreans are proud of K-Pop. But I would take exception to the idea that K-Pop is really that much of a Korean thing, but in large it is a adoption of western cultural entertainment with a intensely commercialized 'cutesy' Korean over-layer slathered on top, which includes a large dose of lithe, writing, scantily clad female bodies and teen idol-boys who look like they are all hopped up on estrogen. The girly-boy aspect isn't very western, but the rest of it all certainly is.

A especially egregious example of Korean performers appropriating western culture is the rap performers here. I understand rap to be an attitudinal expression derived from the complexities of the African American experience in inner cities of America, and very powerfully raw in expressing very particular feelings regarding very specific circumstances uniquely their own. I can imagine SnoopDog's reaction to these Korean pretty boys throwing rap gestures and emulating rap attitudes. Real rappers might feel a bit of comic relief at best, and potentially a bit of outrage at the bastardization of their expressive form. But, that is K-Pop too.

Real Korean music is hauntingly shrill and wholly alien to the western palate. K-Pop is not really Korean, although like I said, it has a shallow layer of Koreanization thinly spread on top. It is really very western, so for a Korean person to jealously lay cultural claim to the art form and be indignant would be the height of myopia, ignorance and ahistoric pride.

CONFUCIUS VS PLATO, AN EXPAT VIEW OF KOREA

Head On Run-in

All Westerners who have experienced more than a few months in Korea have run head-on into Confucius, even though he died about 2,500 years ago. The fact is that much of his philosophy lives on in the modern world in countries like China, Korea, and Vietnam.

Western expats living long-term in Korea tend to feel that the ideas and methods practiced here are quite foreign and unfamiliar to our sentimentality, but in fact, there is a way to find common ground between East and West, even on this thorny subject. That method is by comparing Confucius to Plato.

Comparing Confucius And Plato

Most educated Westerners are familiar, at least in outline, with Plato's thinking, but few were as familiar with Confucius before coming here. In truth, however, they both have a remarkable number of points in common. Let 's just list what some of those general commonalities are:

Plato 1 – Plato was born shortly after the Peloponnesian war, and he was absorbed in achieving a stable peace.
Confucius 1 – Confucius was born shortly after the warring states period in China. He was absorbed in the same way.

Plato 2 – Plato thought that the philosopher should direct the state in optimizing and freezing social norms.
Confucius 2 – Confucius thought exactly the same.

Plato 3 – Plato wanted to use ritual and generational traditionalization to replace governmental enforcement later.
Confucius 3 – Confucius divined the exact same strategy.

Plato 4 – One of Plato's mechanisms was isolationism from contaminating influence.
Confucianism 4 – Isolation and insulation from corrupting influence is built into Confucianism as well.

Plato 5 – None of us would have been comfortable with the society Plato described in The Republic.
Confucius 5 – Aspects of life in Confucian society are uncomfortable even for the adherents.

Plato 6 – Plato's ideas were not widely respected during his lifetime.

Confucius 6 – Confucius tried to find support while he lived, but he died not vindicated in that way.

Plato 7 – Plato's work highlights the trade-off between freedom, and order or peace. Both are desirable but opposed.

Confucius 7 – The order and predictability in Korea society is countered by its strictness and its exclusionist tendency.

Confucius Gets Into Practice

One difference between Plato and Confucius is that Plato never got his experiment into practice, where-as Confucius did. It is, however, important to note that both Plato and Confucius come to us today having proven their incredible irrelevancy resistance over time.

One has to admire the effectiveness of Confucius' strategy in how fundamentally it has gone on working in his absence. The goal of optimizing and freezing politico-social paradigms has been remarkably successful here and in other places as well, preserving a system that is uniform to all citizens for a thousand years. His extreme strain of crafted mono-culture has a militaristic flavor on one hand, but it also provides a bedrock of commonality among Koreans that contributes to the peace and order which we find so pleasant, even in spite of the discomfort that rides along with it.

Glaring Inefficiencies and Exclusion

But even though one admires Confucianism, it has to be said that inefficiencies in practical matters are glaringly apparent. Top down vertical structures of management are seldom effective, and if they ever are, it is only in some narrow, limited manner. Lateral cooperative structures are not only more effective, even in a mono-cultural environment, they are absolutely essential in a multi-cultural scenario. This is one strong reason why integration between Korean and Western populations is so tenuous.

But another reason is the exclusionist aspect of mono-cultures; especial in Confusion strains. All of us can recount dozens of examples of how we have tried to punch below the surface socially here, but have be spit out like a watermelon seed without fail each and every time. The higher we go up in the social structure, the more closed and violent the experience is, and until now there has seemed limited success in attempts to assail that tower.

As original citizens of multi-cultural societies, most expats can see the problems quite clearly, and the differences. The above outline of Plato and Confucius' common points might lead us toward a more conciliatory and empathetic approach to the problem of integration, and begin to assuage some of the frustration that many of us feel on an everyday basis. Perhaps with this ancient comparison we might have an insight tool of commonality, at least in our rational tool box if not in a practical way. But we should mention a bit just on how that tool might be used.

Becoming an Irrelevant Wraith

The typical experience of a mulit-cultural foreigner residing long term in Korea might follow a pattern as follows: The first year is quite positive and hopeful. It is a comfortable community of warm hearted people who make us feel very welcome on the surface, and we may not notice right away that the surface is all the farther we will ever get. It is actually seductively pleasant to exist in a state of quasi anonymity for a time, but then the surrealism of it all begins to wear thin.

The realization that there is no path to integration comes along a year or so into the sojourn. We try many different times to get closer, and we fail dramatically a number of times before it begins to dawn on us that we are socially, politically, and personally irrelevant here. The slow dawning of that realization takes the sharpness out of it, and we settle, more or less passively, into a downward spiral similar to what it might be like to slowly become a wraith; a ghost that leaves no relevancy shadow on the social landscape within which he or she is self inflictedly trapped. Still, we like it enough to stay. It is comfortable enough in other ways to be worth the trade off.

Some people come to terms with the situation and remain healthy in mind and spirit, chipping out a niche of friendships within a small circle. Others fade more and more until they become reclusive, hermit like in their social habits, as though they have completely faded away.

The Long View

One way in which the Platonic comparative can help is simply in providing us with a long view. Korea must change, and indeed it is slowly changing. The power of "The Old Man" is waning as we speak, and the youth are gradually, mostly gently, rejecting and throwing off the chains of the past. In a way there is a nostalgic sorrow to the process because what we love about Korea is beginning to fade in the process, but it is inevitable and necessary that this process of change move on apace. All of us know this already, and re-iterating it here is not necessary other than to build context.

But the long term view is not the only take-away here. We find hints for our own program to expedite change. We know that the keepers of the philosophical flame, (*that is the leaders of society at this point, because they now, rather than Confucius, are charged with overseeing the political/social architecture instead of him*), have to power to let us in. But some event, situation, or circumstance must converge upon them with enough demand in order for them to even consider the sacrilegious move.

Push Toward Relevancy

Another factor that must converge is a push toward relevancy ourselves. If we force a position in which we have obvious apparent value, and we coordinate such a move with such an above described event, situation or circumstance, then the slow change may hasten, and the long view may yet in a shorter term be truncated down to a tractable, comparatively immediate frame.

We don't want to be misunderstood however, to be negative or judgmental toward conservative Korean resistance to multi-cultural relations. Respect for the incredible history here, and love for the culture strictly and naturally prevents that kind of negative sentiment. But opening the gate more to understanding other cultures does not necessitate change within one's own. In fact, in our experience living here we have learned maybe more about our own cultures than we ever knew before. The Korean's who open their hearts to associate more closely with other cultures will certainly gain a deeper appreciation also for their own.

IEK's View on Gangneung

iExperienceKorea's view of Gangneung culture is positive, yet concerned. The Olympics are approaching, and the community is in no way ready. Confucian management paradigms, although instrumental in the development and necessary to the preservation of this uniquely pleasing culture, are slow moving and have yet to jump into full scale preparation for a Global event here in this isolated, mono-cultural, back corner of the world.

• Korea's unique culture has developed because of it's isolation from other cultural influence

• Historically, all of Asia has been geographically isolated from the West, and has developed in sophisticated ways that have been quiet alien to Western sentiments.

• In Korea and Japan, further geographic factors have contributed to further departures in culture. (Japan is on an Island, and Korea on a peninsula.)

• Those isolationist factors have disappeared due to modern globalization in areas like media proliferation, global commerce, information ubiquity, and transportation.

• Philosophical barriers still remain, however, as well as real world experience deficits in Korea's most isolated mono-culture districts.

• Confucianism was designed to isolate and protect unique Asian societies from degradation by outside influence.

• Confucian pre-sets are still very effective in interrupting bi-lateral cultural exchange and cooperation.

• More conservative, more rural districts experience more challenges to non-Korean exchange and cooperation.

• Gangneung's conservative and liberal prominent families story is like a metaphor for the situation.

• Even conservative Foreigners are treated like the liberal family in the story.

• Confucian social order is functionally outdated – designed to freeze society in a pre-industrial agrarian paradigm, although its unique beauty should be preserved as it changes to better fit in the modern world.

• Slow, unchanging agrarian society is a perfect environment for the practice of Confucian principles, because efficiency can easily be sacrificed for the order and relative peace of military style authoritarianism and the inefficient vertical management structures that ride along with Confucius' program.

• Confucius, as practiced in Korea in the modern world, imposes an inefficient top down, vertical hierarchy that is ill-equipped to function in a rapidly changing, multi-cultural, global environment.

• In the West, we must also have top down authoritarian structures to provide order to society.

• We have divided ownership and management authority into two categorical branches, however.

• On one side is responsibility and ownership, which has traditionally been strictly vertical in nature, although alternative structures have been recently taking more of a role.

• The other category is practical, where vertical structures have never worked in a multi-cultural, fast changing world.

We recommend that Korea retain its Confucian structure in its mono-cultural context, but that the governments and residents adopt a more horizontal, collaborative, and inclusive approach when dealing with foreigners. Especially in Gangneung and Pyeongchang, where the Olympics will be held in less than two years.

CONSULTING FOR CORPORATE KOREA ON INTERCULTURAL FRICTION

I have had the unique experience of speaking at high levels about the challenges of carrying authoritarian Confucian management structures into a modern global environment. Many Korean business owners and managers openly admit the problems they have in communicating and problem solving inside their organizations, and even more so when dealing with intercultural teams. They are looking for solutions, and finding them in part through consultation with multiculturally experienced aid.

Inter-Korean Communication Issues

An example is in a Korean Corporation that I consult for now. They recently have included foreign teams on some of their projects and have had difficulties, even project failures, and the CEO wants to find out why. I am embedded into the foreigner project team remotely, and get one set of directives from their Korean lower management teams, but then the CEO tells me what he has directed from the top. Communication does not go down well, and that is part of the company's problem. On the other hand, difficulties at the operational end do not reach up to his level cleanly, so it is hard for him to get the real information he needs to appropriately change his directives, and some of the needed adjustments that fail to be made are critical.

But this communication issue also contributes to the following kind of effects. There are little heroes at the production end, but their efforts and ideas are often co-opted by mid level management. Also, when upper or mid management makes mistakes, the blame is often shifted downward toward the lower strata. Thanks to Confucius, Korean teams resolutely endure this type of injustice, but foreigners only explode when it happens to them, and it does regularly.

Rusty Wheels

In looking for a common causal factor for this and many other similar issues that I can't really outline in a short article, Confucius is a convenient culprit. The overtly authoritarian Confucian stance allows the company to operate in an orderly way in spite of problems and inefficiencies if it operates only in a Korean sphere, but once it reaches out to incorporate non Korean elements on the team, the politics of it just frustrates the foreigners who can't use Confucian politics, and wouldn't use it even if they could for obvious practical reasons. One statement I use with my clients is that politics is rust on the wheels of progress.

Another client I had was an upper management 40 something Korean guy who worked on the sales team of an American company in their Korean branch. His feelings are interesting because he experienced less cultural and language stress in a 100% Korean team, but he feels less responsibility stress when he has to work with a mostly Non-Korean team. In the multicultural settings, he felt much more support and teamwork, and much less competition. Eviscerating himself from all the auxiliary expectations that ride along with Confucian hierarchy was an incredibly liberating experience for him, even though he loves Korean culture and also recognizes its beauty and strengths, as do I. Shirking the politics on the production side allowed team efficiency to go up to a level that shocked him the first time he experienced it.

Patience and Sensitivity

These experiences are ONLY from KOREAN PEOPLE who are having trouble with reverse integration. Time would fail me if I tried to describe the feelings of some of the foreigner teams that I have worked with in this same capacity. Let me just say the attrition rate is high without a lot of intervention, at least during the first six months until Korean systems can begin to adapt some multi-cultural sensitivity, and the foreigners, some greater patience. In Seoul, this process has been going on for decades, and continues with many success stories, along with a lot of growing pains on both sides.

I absolutely love the peace and predictability that the Korean social order brings to society, and judge it very positively on that metric, while at the same time I am very critical of many developments in my own home country. I like it here better overall, and rue the time when the unique, exotic beauty of the isolated, protected culture begins to fade away. I truly hope that Korea can learn lessons from other Cultures whose uniqueness has been gradually flattened by radical adoption of the ubiquitous global culture. While multicultural cooperation is necessary, and the philosophical factors that cause friction must be discussed and addressed, I truly hope that Korea's intercultural efforts amount to skillful adaptation and accommodation, and not to loss of its beauty and strength in change.

I respect Confucius and the success he has achieved in his purposeful aim to architect, isolate, and protect his uniquely defined concept of what a society should be. At the same time, however, I don't think it an insult to him to call his methods alone outdated and inadequate for the 2018 world environment. Korea is changing radically because it HAS too, not because of any one person or group that really thinks it should. I really hope as that happens that this culture will remain distinct and retain it's beauty.

CONSERVATISM IN A LIBERAL WORLD

The West has a history in its fight against conservative strangle holds that dampen needed change. Bastions of conservative tradition come in a long list. From the Catholic Dark Ages, to the Divine Right of Kings, violent revolution has often been the result of authoritarian resistance to change. The Reformation Period along with the American and French Revolutions serve to highlight lessons of reactionary forces building to a breakout point under the pressure of conservative resistance to explosive change.

On the other hand, defenders of Conservatism, like Edmond Burke and Joseph DeMaistre point toward rapid change as the cause of social destabilization rather than the effect of pent up pressure to change. Conservative theories tend to discount the pressure cooker factor in change resistant situations. Burke especially made the case that change must come from within the historical context of a culture if the lid on violent revolution is to be kept safely in place. Pure Burkean Conservatives are not opposed to change, but want it to happen slowly through peaceful bureaucratic means.

Balancing Social Stability and Needed Change

There is an interesting dichotomy in perspective here that looms large as a potential lens through which to view Korean management of conservative social change. And Korea is not the only architect of a moderate transition into the modern era of rapid flux and change. Asia in general has a traditional reverences of the past, and that has served her for thousands of years in the area of stability and resistance to change. And it seems to be benefiting Asian cultures still as they face the quickening erosion of the age old cultures in the quickening flow of change and cultural confluence in the modern world.

It seems as though Korea has been successful in balancing the pressure demand for change with a careful patience that has kept its population grounded in its historic roots until now. But on the threshold of the generation gap, the young generation, egged on by the invasion Western values and ideas, is more and more restless under the authoritarian thumb of conservative guardians.

Another force that pushes strong against Korea's conservative values is the opening of international travel and business activity both inside and out of Korea. The

1980s was the decade that Koreans first began to travel, and then only the elite in society could do so. But with the financial strain of the IMF crisis in the 1990s, Korean conservative protectorate was obliged to welcome in more foreign interest and the influence that came along with it.

iExperienceKorea is based in Gangneung City, the location of the upcoming 2018 Winter Olympic games. The foreigners here, myself included, have found a refuge of conservative Confucian Korea that has not been much exposed to cultural contamination, and retains a strong strain of ancient, exotic Korea.

Appreciating the Beauty of Old Korea

When foreigners flood into the area, they are in for an unexpected treat if they are respectful of the people and their ways. Rural Koreans are indescribably hospitable, but can be quite reserved and a bit shy. Most of our Gangneung neighbors have not had any experience whatsoever with any culture other than their own; at least besides what they get from Hollywood.

Conservatism is fading in the West, and massive changes are afoot. Globalization and cultural homogeny are far advanced in many parts of the world. This delicate flower of ancient culture still retains many of the views and perspectives that it has held for thousands of years. The East Coast of Korea is a fascinating microcosm of Conservative values set like a gem nesting at the edge of the modern world.

MINORITY / MAJORITY RELATIONS

South Africa, the United States, Israel, and many other countries have notorious issues with minority / majority relations, and much academic focus has gone into the issue from the time of colonialism until now. Enough research has gone into the subject to make it a subset of more than one discipline, but a few points out of the systematized theoretical consensus can serve well as a conceptual tool for anyone dealing with multi-cultural situations.

In many situations, the minority group is in tension with the majority due to negative perceptions and friction between them. America has the African American community, along with the Hispanic community as case studies, in addition to an incredible field of less populous minority communities living together with the majority white European masses. *(Sidebar: The Hispanic population is no longer considered a minority in the US).* In South Africa however, the privileged group is not the majority, as was the case in many regions under the colonial British Crown in days gone by.

Negative Perceptions

The dynamics are quite different as the situations differ, and it is enlightening to think about these case studies structurally, looking for common variations that concombinantly influence each other in flux. For example, when the minority is negatively viewed by the majority, it begins in many ways to negatively view itself, and the desire to be accepted into the majority group exists in tension with the anger toward that group. In that situation, there are always examples of super-achievers who are able to integrate to high levels of influence in the majority group, and these are held as heroes in the minority group, and as examples to aspire too, but those are the exceptional cases, and following that light only leads the mass of the minority into more disappointment and frustration in the long run.

Positive Perceptions

When the situation is reversed however, and the minority is positively viewed by the majority, bubbles of tolerance, and even appreciative integration are created where the minority group members feel respected by the majority, and less internal and external conflict and tension ensue.

In Korea, Western foreigners have a place as English teachers at the fringes of society, and in high level business and foreign relations can participate in roles at a more engaged level. Korea's history of exclusionist policy has yet to dissipate enough to create much "non-

Korean" space in the society, but America has been struggling with the African American issue for a couple hundred years, and still fails to set a golden example in minority / majority comfort and cooperation. Korea by contrast, *(admitting that the historical foundation upon which Korean and Western relations is based is much more pedestrian and positive than that of the slavery history in the US case),* is quite accommodating in allowing Western minority residents a comfortable niche on the fringes of the socio-political-commercial world.

REORIENTING RESPECT IN KOREAN SOCIETY

Reorienting On A Child's Level

I have the privilege of tutoring young boys privately here, and there is an interesting pattern that often repeats when a young Korean boy first engages with a non-Korean, Western teacher; at least in my experience.

- At first they are shy.
- Then they relax because the authority seems to be gone from the situation.
- Then they go crazy, testing all the boundaries that they can (which is a little boy's primary job in life).
- Then I have to gently leave the class early one time because they have gradually gotten totally out of hand.
- Then, when I come the next time to class, we understand each other and have a couple or few years of really good classes.

Reorienting On An Adult's Level

Interestingly, I have experienced something similar in the adult Korean community among friends and work associates.

- At first they feel liberated because I don't fit into their structure.
- Then they begin to unknowingly do things that seem a bit disrespectful compared to how they would treat another Korean.
- Then I kindly talk with them about how I perceive the changing relationship dynamics.
- Then they adjust and we have a good relationship moving forward.

In some cases, I think that living in a strict authoritarian society creates potential for a period of orientation imbalance when that structure is first removed in early exposure to non-Korean situations. But I am always impressed by how quickly most Koreans figure out the situation and adjust.

I have to say though, that coming from a society that has less in the way of authority structures, there seems to be much more potential among some Westerners for general disrespectful behavior, and much less potential for adjustment.

THE WHITE MAN'S BURDEN

In 1900, most of Asia was in a state of Feudalism that had not really changed for a thousand years. It consisted of a historically dominated mindset, not in any way progressive. It was similar to Europe before Isaac Newton and Francis Bacon began the program of turning the West around to face a progressive future. We have since then adopted a careful mix of rationalism and empiricism that underpins the scientific method. This in turn has led the West to a pinnacle of descriptive knowledge of the natural world that is rich in benevolent application, although our knowledge has not been applied always in a beneficial way. It has a darker side.

Prior to the Enlightenment, Europe was mostly dominated by a backward facing paradigm constipated by outdated traditional mindsets and illogical Machiavellian systems of authority that kept threatening to crush the limping process of bringing Europe out of the dark ages. Romantic reactionary thinkers like Byron and Shelly, who hearkened back nostalgically to the medieval agrarian world, at the same time would not have enjoyed the comfort deficit they would have experienced living in a 14th or 15th century society, and neither would we. We may complain about the downside of modern progressiveness, but we do so in a state of great physical comfort. Dentistry, for example, is a nice benefit of living in the modern world, and so are smart phones.

Colonial Audacity

There was a time when Europeans, in the throes of prideful Colonial audacity, portrayed their exploitive domination of the 3rd world as a kind of gift; a blessing that the superior white man was bringing to the inferior races. The fact is, however, that the ravages which resulted are painful for fair-minded, informed people to recount today.

Now, with the modern capitalistic system teetering on the edge of failure after having harvested a unbelievable percentage of the rich resources of this wealthy planet, and having succeeded in the monumental project of burning up those resources nearly within one century, some careful thinkers have concluded that Byron and Shelly were correct in their agrarian sentiments, and that progress by a Western definitive turned out to not be progress after all.

Benefits of Knowledge and Danger of Prideful Management

The author of this article, however, would like to draw a distinction between the benefits of more knowledge and the danger of prideful management. The knowledge that has been brought into the world by Western Modern Rational Empiricism cannot really be successfully dismissed. And it was through the Western tradition that this powerful apparatus came to birth and fruition. But unfortunately, what was also born in SOME through that process was an irrational ethnic pride and a will to dominate through the power that rides with science. This has turned much of the benefit of positive scientific developments often to heinous outcomes.

Mr. Rudyard Kipling's neological phrase, "The White Man's Burden." may have been wrongfully applied to European rulership and the dominance of the Earth, but it may have at one time been applicable to the knowledge acquiring apparatus of the scientific method. Actually, helping other nations to come around to improvements in data analysis might better be portrayed as an honor than a burden. But now, even that can no longer be claimed as either the honor or the burden of the West alone.

It was not through superiority of intellect or some ethno-racial giftedness that knowledge first lifted itself from the dust of ignorant millenniums in Europe. Rather, it was through the uniqueness of Western history, together with the luck of the times, mixed with the blood of millions, that brought the power of science first there. Indeed, the spark had flickered in India, Persia, Chaldea, and China at least, not only in Greece, and there is no doubt that it would have burst into flame again somewhere if it had not done so in Europe first.

Asia has come into the programs of the modern world with a vengeance during the second half of the 20th Century, and the old diminutive attitudes toward her, and the entire the 3rd world for that matter, have proven over time to be absolutely bankrupt. Frankly, even the term "3rd world", aside from its colloquial utility, holds potentially judgmental connotations *(drawing a distinction now between positive pre-modern cultural values and negative prideful management)*. For someone to claim that the IEK holds to those despicable attitudes would be to make an egregious false accusation indeed.

LANGUAGE ISSUES FOR IMMIGRANTS TO KOREA

It must be said that some people have the gift of language, either because of some intellectual propensity, or simply because they can more easily take the regular time necessary to overcome the inherent conceptual resistance involved in learning a new form of thinking and speech. For most of us, however, taking the time is a major challenge, and the natural ability is simply not up to the task of learning without the steady schedule commitment.

A few foreigners who have lived in Korea long term have picked up the language passably, but the truth is that most have not truly done so, even after 5 or ten years. Why not? Why have most not taken the time to do it? We fall under criticism, and sometimes under angry attack for the failure, and I myself, as one of the miserable culprits, feel the need to speak in defense of myself at least. I hope others in the sheepish position that I find myself in can relate to the following points.

Global Language

First of all, it is a both a blessing and a curse to have one's indigenous language be the current global standard. Some of my counterparts have made the observation that although some Korean people get a bit miffed at us when we don't speak Korean, at the same time, most Koreans have been studying English for 30 years and are still not functional. Without reference to the exceptional cases, most people who have really learned a language fluently have done so by being thrown into a situation where they are forced to use it. So Koreans are in a similar situation with us lame foreigners in that regard. Being able to default to an easier means of communication *(in their case, Korean)* allows the path of least resistance law to take hold, and we all have an out *(in our case, English)*.

Even though most Koreans are not comfortable with English, they know enough to be understood by us, and to make themselves understood using English. This makes the motive for us to learn Korean less pressing, and allows us to postpone the strict effort till the next year, and the next, and the next...

This having been said, I took an energetic crack at Korean when I first moved here and learned more than 500 words that I thought would help me. Then I found out that the written words and the spoken words were different. My bubble didn't pop, but it lost some air.

Ambiguity Intolerance

So I tried taking a class with foreign wives, and found that classes being taught to East Asian students were being handled with a level of ambiguity that a structurally educated Western mind had a hard time assimilating. Of course, having never been through rigorous schooling, most of the East Asian students in that class would not easily have been able to adjust to a Western educational approach either.

Strict Memorization

But the strict memorization methods of Korean teaching are hard for me to follow also, as I want to understand the language rules and learn that way instead of have huge lists of vocabulary pushed at me at a pace that almost crushes my small brain. That is the Korean way, and they are shockingly adept at memorization, but it too doesn't mesh well with the way I have always learned from youth on up in America. It is hard to adjust.

A Humbling Experience

A final difficulty stems I think from the way that Koreans themselves have learned English. They are often afraid to speak less than perfect English and sometimes miss communication opportunities because they know their expressions won't be grammatically perfect. I believe that this hypersensitivity to grammar error crosses over and contributes to the way most Koreans respond when I try to speak my broken Korean. Rather than focusing to understand what I am trying to say, it usually turns into a lecture on how bad, or jokes about how funny my clunky attempts are. I can laugh at myself, but not all the time. That type of response lets more air out of the bubble.

My wife tells me I am not humble enough, which I suppose is a more simple way to express all of the above. Learning a language is always going to be a humbling experience.

PROBLEM SOLVING VERSUS PROBLEM MANAGEMENT

By age *(which is one of the most important measures in Korea)* I am the middle member of a seven member oversight committee in a management role over a Korean organization with 25 to 30 members all told. As the only foreigner in the group, I have learned much acting in this role over the past 6 or 7 years. There is a incredible difference in the way that the two cultures approach problems.

Where is The Plan?

I initially got a hint of a diametric Korean method during my first year living here. I had a desire back then to cooperate with a university in a project involving a program that the school already had running, and I went there seeking information about their effort. I was surprised to find out that even though a large collective effort was underway, they had no written plan that they were working from to guide it, or to inform others about it. This caused me a great deal of confusion at first, until a friend stepped in to explain.

He told me about the power of the social movement in Korea, and that plans are not as necessary here as is having a social footprint. The alumni from your grade school is one of the most powerful and important elements of social capital that Korean people can acquire, but it is just one of many. If you want to do something, you call in the assistance of your social machinery to make it happen, and then it simply does.

To say there is no plan is hyperbolic, because a plan obviously does exist, but often, the plan is largely just a mental thing, conveyed verbally, and only loosely followed. This is not to say that plans are without merit or import here, but that they are not the primary or most important tool in the shed. Actually, if a more formal plan does make it onto the board, it can be followed by Korean machinery with such powerful focus that it can be detrimental, because it may never be adjusted to meet ongoing changes as they come into view, where-as a looser structured plan can do that.

Social Politics as a Strength, Not a Weakness?

In the body where I function, there are three older Korean gentlemen, and three who are younger than me. If I try to identify a problem to the older ones, it can easily be viewed as criticism of their authority, and negative ramifications can ensue. If I turn to the younger three members and speak of problems, the potential for stepping on toes is even more delicate. So what happens is that I have learned to keep quiet and watch as problems go unaddressed year after year. There seems to be a political side to not having a committed plan in place as well.

To a Western mind, this is anathema, and for a long while, it really bothered me. But as time has passed, I have learned to respect the power of the social capital in place. People in operational positions are not distracted by problems, and they continue resolutely to operate at an acceptable level of efficiency *(by slower Korean standards)* even in spite of what I still instinctively view as significant, even crippling problems. Why does the Korean system still work? Because the operators are held in place by a social order that is so strong, the plan becomes secondary to the structure, and consequently, so do the problems, and so does the efficiency.

Having said this, it obviously would be much more comfortable and profitable if the problems were solved, but I have to wonder if solving the problems efficiently, like a Western minded person would do, might not in fact sometimes break other things that are more delicate and important in the long run, not only here, but also back home. Maybe, even though fewer things are fixed with a problem management approach, with a problem solving approach is it possible that more things end up getting broken? The jury is still out in my *'trying to be open'* mind.

KOREAN VALUES – FROM WHENCE DO THEY COME?

For those of us who have made Korea our alien home, we have always been impressed by the values that the culture and society hold dear.

Some Key Korean Values

- Family Life
- Industriousness
- Education
- Dignity
- Respect
- Kindness
- Knowing Ones Place and Staying in it

These are just some of more we could enumerate. Where do these admirable traits come from, and why are they so deeply ingrained in everyone who lives here? In short, the answer is Confucius.

The Principle of Li

Confucius was a scholar of history and ethics, but that was not all. He also wanted to restore peace and order to a society that was being torn apart by civil war. In order to do this, he taught a principle known as Li, which basically dictates everyone's role in society, and then strictly expects them to know it and to keep it.

Actually, Li had two levels of meaning. The first is a definitive level of meaning; **propriety, courtesy, and order in all things**. The second is a set of preservative measures meant to keep the structure in place; **ritual, ceremony, and reverence**.

The following is a quotation from a translation from "The Analects"

Of all things that people live by, Li is the greatest. Without Li, we do not know how to conduct a proper worship of the spirits of the universe; or how to establish the proper status of the king and his ministers, the ruler and the ruled, the elders and the juniors; or how to establish the moral relationships between the sexes, between parents and children, and between brothers; or how to distinguish the different degrees of relationships in the family. That is why a gentleman chun-tzu (Junsa) holds li in such high regard.

The Principle of Jen (ren)

A second principle that governs the expression of Li was Jen (ren). Jen involves how the Junsa should carry out his social relations, with "HUMAN-HEARTEDNESS", which is one translation of the word Jen. If Li deals with rules, then Jen deals with the inner nature of a human. It entails the belief that human nature is inherently good, and that self-cultivation will bring that goodness out in fuller measure.

Mencius (one of Confucius' foremost disciples) taught that education and knowledge are the keys to this type of critical self cultivation, especially in the fields of history and ethics.

The following is a quotation from a translation of "The Great Learning"

When true knowledge is achieved, then the will becomes sincere; when the heart is set right, then the personal life is cultivated; when the personal life is cultivated, the family life is regulated; when the family life is regulated, then the national life is orderly; and when the national life is orderly, then there is peace in the world. From the Emperor down to the common men, all must regard the cultivation of the personal life as the root or foundation.

So Confucian thought teaches that Li will make everyone behave in the right way, and Jen will make everyone treat everyone else kindly.

THE HUMAN FACTOR IN KOREA

We all know that the most difficult factors to measure in any situation are the subjective ones. In Western paradigms of judgment, we try to take feelings into account in our own way. In Korea, there seems to be a bit of a difference.

The Fender Bender Story

I had a little fender bender last winter, where a Korean woman was parked and ready to pull out. I was slowly driving past in the parking lot when she pulled out and tapped the side of my car. That caused about w300,000 won *(about $300.00)* in damage. She hadn't seen me because she had failed to scrape the snow off her side windows. She simply couldn't see.

She was quite distraught, mostly because she feared upsetting her husband who showed up later. He turned out to be a rather stern type, and steadily gave her the evil glare throughout the rest of the episode. But the police started out telling her that it was her fault. Upon getting this feedback, she went into an emotional tirade. Long story short, the Police ended up changing their analysis based on her emotional response. They blamed me for 30% of the fault. I felt sorry for her too, so I didn't protest the change.

In America, the Police would have been sympathetic to the woman's emotions (hopefully). However, the situational justice would have taken precedent over the emotion. It is just the way we see things. In Korea, the subjective emotion of the parties in a situation seems to have more bearing on judicial outcomes.

The Street Market Story

Another situation happened in the street market. A long time vendor had been in long term posession of a sales space, and had gotten older. She came to her stall less and less, so the City began leasing the space to someone else. The elderly Korean woman objected by coming early one day, and laying down in the stall so that no one else could set up there. This initiated a visit by the City representatives, and matters were adjusted to accommodate her.

Once again, in America things would have been handled differently. If the woman would have remained laying there, the police would have come and forcibly removed her. What is more, most people would have applauded the stricter action.

To a Westerner, the Korean way of approaching an emotional situation can seem quite disorienting at first. But I have actually been the recipient of such sensitivity myself a number of times in the past. Although I didn't indulge in an emotional display, my pitiable situational estate drew accommodation from kind hearted bureaucrats.

Chewy in The Middle

I recall a **Far Side** comic where two polar bears are standing over an igloo, and the ice house has a bite taken out of it. One polar bear is saying to the other, "Crunchy on the outside. Chewy on the inside." Korean people can be that way too. They can be a bit abrupt on the outside, but underneath, most have quite a soft heart.

Here is some good advice in dealing with Korean resistance to reasonable requests. If at first you get a no, ask again in a polite, sincere manner. It won't work every time, but usually, the third or fourth time, their inherent compassion will burn through their PaliPali *(hurry, hurry)* exterior.

COMPARING INTEGRATION IN OPEN VERSUS ISO-CULTURES

We talk a lot within iExperienceKorea about iso-cultures and open cultures. A set of specific sensitivities is involved in addressing these issues, however, because there are often painful episodes attached to integration experiences on both sides.

There Is No Cultural Vacuum

People who come from multi-cultural backgrounds do not exist in a cultural vacuum themselves. My mother, for example, was from a Welsh heritage, while my father's family was from Germany. Living in a multi-cultural community did not mean that the roots of my family heritage were totally pulled out. The rules of respect and the value systems that we held to inside the walls of our home were specific to our particular European backgrounds. Many of our neighbors had radically different ways of seeing and doing things in comparison to us, just as we did compared to them.

We did not view the differences as necessarily right or wrong, but only as different. If open culture citizens think of our neighbors judgmentally in that way, any open culture community will end up only tearing itself apart.

Wherever there are differences there are going to be discomforts, but most multi-cultural interactions occur in quite a conciliatory way.

It Takes Two Generations

We don't mean to paint over the difficulties with first and second generation immigrants to the US, or to other open cultures, because there are undeniable problems there in those first two generations. But those involve "closed culture" people learning to adjust to open cultures.

We cannot ignore the long term issues regarding race relations in open cultures either. But truthfully, most of the everyday people you live with in the States manage an incredible level of peaceful, productive integration in the workplace, at school, and in the neighborhoods at large. We are very open minded to different ways of thinking and doing things. As mentioned above, we have to be or our societies wouldn't work as well as they do. But still, it takes a couple of generations for many iso-cultural immigrants to settle in, and the children of immigrants often have a difficult time reconciling the differential between their parent's ongoing isolation, and their integration.

Joining a CLOSED Culture is Harder

If the friction and pain involved in moving to an open culture is harsh, then what of the problems for a multi-cultural, or a different mono-cultural immigrant trying to find a place in a new, strict iso-culture? Are there ways in which that experience could be even more difficult than going to an open one?

An open culture is open, after all, and accepting of other people's ways. They have practical means of working with and accommodating people from other lands, along with a lot of experiences doing so. Closed cultures, however, are by definition closed. The social machinery in a mono-culture is designed specifically to reject different ideas and ways of seeing or doing things.

I have been criticized and abused for pointing this out in the past, but the truth of it remains. Countries like Korea, who have entered into the world community and who invite foreigners here for business and family interactions, are feeling the need to make more allowances in order to provide a little more room for those from other cultures to attain some comfort and acceptance here. I think they also have a responsibility to do better.

Understanding Others Doesn't Mean Being Exactly Like Them

When I was young, my home had a specific culture that was dear to me. Being understanding and kind to other people did not mean I had to give up my culture. Immigrants to Korea can't ask Koreans to do that. But how fair is it to ask an immigrant to entirely change to become a Korean? That would not only be unfair, it would be impossible.

I know that Koreans can open their hearts and minds to foreigners better in that way too. It will take more time, and more experience together, but the process doesn't have to be viewed as a challenge to Korean culture. And neither does making the recommendation.

DO YOU KNOW HOW TO TAKE OFF YOUR SHOES – KOREAN STYLE?

A large number of foreigners are coming to Gangneung, Pyeongchang, and Jeongson. There will be quite a number who stay in Korean homes during the 2018 Winter Olympics. The potential for rich inter-cultural experience is highest in the home stay setting, but there are some differences we should all keep in mind.

Think Close to The Floor

Korean people live much of their lives on the floor. Especially in rural areas, a home might have a chair or two, but many families still sit on the floor with low tables for meals. Is it any wonder that shoes are not worn in the home?

And yet, there is a simple method of taking off your shoes that might not be easily perceived. Actually, some of my Western friends who have lived here many years still don't quite get it right. But think about this…

The Place Where Shoes are Happy

The little area where we take off our shoes in a Korean home or restaurant, is crowded up right close to the entry door. Usually, there are a bunch of shoes jumbled up there, waiting to be used. But that area is full of shoe dirt from outside. What happens if you take off your shoes, and step in that shoe dirt with your socks? Doesn't that entirely defeat the purpose? Let's all nod our heads.

The Korean Shoe Hop

Korean people won't say anything if we take off our shoes that way, but they will cringe inside. A soon as you leave, most Korean home-makers will go about cleaning the entire floor. The best way to do it is to loosen both shoes so that you are standing in them on your toes, and then hop lightly up onto the clean, inner floor area without touching the shoe area floor with your socks.

THE KOREAN STOIC VS THE WESTERN ROMANTIC

The Modern Self

We find in the Western consciousness a quite modern view of the self that did not manifest until the dramatic increase in writing and the proliferation of the written record. In the expressions of thinkers like James Boswell and Jean Jacques Rousseau there is a rather clean departure from the bonds of a socially imposed self portraiture. It was an outbreak of freedom and loneliness in a new kind of self concept. This new *'self view'* is idyllically encapsulated in the model of the romantic hero.

The Romantic Hero

The romantic hero was someone in contrast with the classical hero, because he was able to shirk completely all the restrictions that society would seek to impose upon him. The classical hero would endure hardship and death. He was resolute to bear the "Star Trek" burden, where "the needs of the many outweigh the needs of the few". The romantic hero, by contrast, was only true to himself. He lived a life of existential angst and often died young in the throes of some self indulgent passion.

Our Own Intellectual History

In only a preliminary exposure to Western intellectual history, we see the development of the romantic hero. That development has had true impact on the way we see the world; breaking new ground, being bohemian, avant-garde, and only *(or at least primarily),* true to one's self. I was shocked in comparing the difference between someone like Samuel Johnson, who was so preoccupied with the strictures of a "proper" life, in his tirades against Voltaire, who conversely struck out so much against the established norms. That shock came because, in my heart, and in the hearts of most Westerners I know, the ghost of the romantic lurks. It is taunting us to be different, to strike out into new territory, and to live our passions apart from responsibility to anyone or anything else.

And then I moved to Korea. The dignity of the Old Korean Man has a definite powerful impact on someone who has been unknowingly bit by a historical tradition of romanticism. While I consider myself as having been steady and responsible in my life, many of the Korean guys I know are like a rock in some comparative ways. So many of these guys grew up in abject poverty and deprivation with no way up and out of it other than through the strict limitations of a ritualistic, tradition bound system. The boundaries within which they could operate were so strict in comparison to anything any modern Westerner could imagine. There is a respect due there than cannot be denied.

The More Admirable Species of Man

Respect in the West is bifurcated. There are those guys who get a job and stay at it for 40 years before retiring, and who have been steady in a way similar to that of a Korean grandfather. But truthfully, the self made man who strikes out on his own path, blazing a new trail to his own brand of success, is maybe the more admirable species of Western man.

While both the romantic and the stoic have their own qualities to admire, it seems to me that the West emphasizes the romantic, and the East, the stoic. And maybe that is why most of what is new in the world comes from the West.

It is true that discovery is painful, costly, and often leads to uncontrolled, even deadly outcomes. René de Chateaubriand and Victor Hugo taught us that with their fictional romantic heroes, and Jim Morrison, Janice Joplin, James Dean, and Kurt Cobain continue to vitalize the lesson. I guess that old Korean guys epitomize the stoic brand of a respectable man.

PERSONAL SPACE AND PHYSICAL INTERACTION IN KOREA

The state of Washington in North West USA is about the same size in land mass as the entire South Korean peninsula. But the population is still under ten million; less than 20% of the number of people who live in Korea. Of course, this has an impact on our sense of personal space.

The Old Style Korean Pusher Man

In the early 1990's, when I first visited Korea, they still had the yellow shirt guys. If you don't remember, they were the ones who pushed the crowd of people more tightly into the subway to make more room for more to get in. It was not so bad for me because I'm tall, but I felt a little sorry for the ajama (*middle aged Korean woman*) who's head got crammed into my armpit. But oddly to me at the time, she didn't seem to mind.

While you might find a differential in personal space perspective between any crowded VS non crowded area, there are other, more interesting ways in which personal space interactions in Korea may seem a bit odd at first.

Help Up the Stairs

On the stairs in the subway station, an older Korean man probably thought I was going too slow. I am guessing about that, but the clue was his forearm across the small of my back pushing me up the stairs at a faster pace. If it wasn't for the surprise, I might consider that a favor. But that kind of contact was really strange to me the first time.

I Don't Know You, But I Know You

I think that Korean people have commonality together on levels that Westerners don't really comprehend. It is not only a convention when they call strangers "Brother", "Sister", or "Uncle". It is a feeling that they really share together, even if they've never met each other before. Maybe that is reflected in the physical familiarity they feel toward strangers as well. It is not unusual to see a couple of Korean strangers sitting on the subway, and one guy might be sleeping with his head resting on another guys shoulder.

The Hustle Along

A final interesting experience is between men. A Korean guy grabs you by your arm and forcibly compels you along a path. Sometimes it is out the door. Sometimes it's to the buffet line. It may be to some other destination that he thinks you want to go. It is a common behavior among men, (*I don't know if women do it to each other*). Apparently is it a sign of affectionate warmth to do so. Frankly, I was missunderstandably almost offended the first time it happened to me. But I know now that it is just one more difference in how Korean people view personal space and physical interaction.

DON'T STEP ON MY NUN-CHI! – KOREAN SENSITIVITY TO FEELINGS

He says, "I'll never understand women." She says, "Men are impossible to understand." We have all heard these complaints, and most of us have expressed them ourselves. But understanding requires an open mind. Do statements like those above indicate openness, or something else?

Men and women are different, and that is why understanding doesn't always come naturally. But both genders are logical (usually) in our own ways. Listening with an open mind and asking questions about what we don't' understand is the key. Unfortunately, closing our minds is a reflex that we have to fight.

A Greater Challenge

Truthfully, this article is not only about understanding the opposite sex, which is admittedly sometimes a challenge. A greater challenge can be to understand a different culture, or for someone from a different culture to understand us. The truth is that as soon as we make some kind of hard judgment, we stop ourselves from listening and learning. Being judgmental is the worst course in the development of an understanding spirit.

Pain and irritation can often cause us to close our minds, get angry, and become judgmental. But in many cases, if we open our minds and try to understand, we would find that we really don't need to be irritated. We might not need to feel any pain in the first place.

Communication is hard though, but it is necessary if we want to understand differences and see things through the eyes of others. There are many impediments to good communication, and language is certainly one of them. But it might be said that a closed mind, pain, and prejudice are even worse blockages.

NUN-CHI Means "Don't Cause Pain"

Koreans have a concept called NUN-CHI, which they are taught from a young age. Basically, it means they have to be sensitive to others feelings. They are taught to communicate with long, round-about, half obscure terms that a Westerner would call, "Beating Around the Bush". But actually, it is a kind of 'hyper-tact'. The other side of NUN-CHI is that the listener has to understand WITHOUT the explicitness of a painful, overly emotional delivery. NUN-CHI facilitates dignity all around, which is a quality of high value to Koreans.

We might tell our Korean friends that they don't have to practice NUN-CHI with us, and that might be true.

What we should try not to forget, however, is that we can't behave toward them without some NUN-CHI. We can't expect to be blunt with Koreans the same way we sometimes are with each other, and still have good results. Remember, if we cause pain, then even though we keep an open mind, they will have a hard time. The result will be continued lack of understanding after all.

There is another perspective on NUN-CHI too. Think of this. If others are being obscure and sensitive about what they say and how they say it, what do we have to do in response? We have to listen more carefully, and even ask questions for clarity. It just follows. And better listening with good questions can only be good for understanding.

In the end, it seems that being blunt might not be the best way to communicate, but that taking some courses in NUN-CHI might even help in our relationships with the opposite sex.

WHY DO SOME KOREAN PEOPLE THINK THEIR CULTURE IS ALL MESSED UP?

I have spoken to many Korean people on this subject, and a lot of people have mixed feelings about it. Older people are proud of their culture, and want to preserve it, while younger people feel that it is inefficient in the modern world, sometimes illogical, and often burdensome.

For the latter, the authority system is a cause of a lot of problems. They don't like the hierarchy and the hyper-politicization of social relationships. You can't talk openly to people who are older than you without worrying about some kind of backlash, and this causes subtle issues in any social group, from the family, to the class room, to the workplace, and even among friends.

Another interesting nuance of the culture is the accounting that goes on. Everyone does tit for tat, and tries to keep relationship investment balanced, but in Korea it is strictly codified, and there is always this question of whether or not some act of kindness was a manipulative move with all kinds of strings attached.

Younger Koreans carry the expectations of the entire older generation on their shoulders. They get pushed around, blamed when something goes wrong (*even when it isn't their fault*) and otherwise have to eat dirt and at the same time bite their tongues. In the past, with less insight into different cultures, Korean people felt this situation was normal, and they just waited until they got older in order to escape those pressures and join the ranks of the dominators instead. Now, through comparative insight into more relaxed Western cultural paradigms, some seem less satisfied with the Korean status quo and are gently forcing some change.

AM I A TEACHER OR JUST A CONVERSATION OPPORTUNITY?

Many Western foreigners now in Korea (maybe most) are here as English Teachers. Among these, there are a few different kinds. One type of teacher works at Universities, and interacts with an older group of students. Another group works with elementary and middle school students before they enter high school. This second group can work either at the private academies, or at the public schools.

Temporary Teachers

In both categories of teachers mentioned above, there are a larger percentage of people who are here only for a one or two year contract, but who plan a short stay and then go home. They are usually younger (20-30 something) and are still in a bit of a party mode while trying to pay off student loans.

Permanent Teachers

The smaller percentage is people who have actually developed roots here, either because they married into the culture, they are more comfortable here for some reason, or they really love Korea. Of course, there can be a mix of those motives too.

Regardless of which type of teacher, the Korean education system seems a bit divided in relation to its inclusion of foreign teachers. In most accounts (*correct me if I'm wrong*) the Korean teachers handle grammar, listening, reading, writing and speaking in the formal, school related context, and foreign teachers are more for less formal conversation practice.

Korean Education System – Takes Time To Learn It

It is understandable that short term, one year teachers are really not in a good position to interface with the Korean education structure well, since they don't really have much time to learn how it works, and are not really teachers by trade in the first place. Most are architects, accountants, journalism majors, or an eclectic mix of differently focused people. And real English interaction is what is truly missing in Korea. Conversationalists are really needed.

On the other hand, for those of us who are actually here teaching long term, it may be nice to gain some traction in other ways in order to be viewed as offering little more long term relevance. For example, I teach mostly private students because I really love the kids. It is hard to have quality time with a group, but one on one, you can really have a granular relationship with them. So I am able to teach math, science, computer programming, graphic arts, music, and English, all of it both inside and outside the boundaries of their school curriculum.

But I also know teachers who work in institutional settings who can't seem to crash through the conversational ceiling pre-set. Congratulations to the few that have done so, and encouragement to those of us who still want to try. Outside the institutional setting, it is easier for me to do more than just conversation. But inside, it still might be hard.

THE SHOULDERS ON WHICH WE STAND – THE ENGLISH TEACHERS WHO CAME BEFORE

There are two different layers of Korean experience. iExperienceKorea is interested in both. One layer is the social one. This is where we have informal friendships, and enjoy having a good time together. The second layer is more formal, where we need to actually work together with some kind of oversight dimension involved. This happens with western foreigners mostly in scholastic circumstances, and not much outside of the educational field.

Informal Social Experience

Informal social interactions are maybe more comfortable in Korea than they are in the West. Koreans are kind, thoughtful, and hospitable to a degree that is hard to describe. Other cultures are that way too. African and South American societies are well known for the warmth and affection. But in Korea there is a kind of dignity combined with a certain energy and productivity that gives the Korean experience a different, powerful impact in its expression.

Formal Oversight Interactions

Formal interactions however, have had a history of being more exclusive an difficult for foreigners to experience. In the educational field, the notorious "Bad Employer" stories are becoming fewer and fewer. For Native Speaker Teachers who were not here 10 or 15 years ago, working under a Korean management system in an EDUCATION setting can feel quite accommodating. It is similar now to how informal, social interactions feel. That was not the case a decade or two ago. It is nice to see that working together for 30 years has resulted in a comfortable place for foreigners who teach in Academies, Elementary Schools, Middle Schools, and Universities.

It strikes me that most foreigners here now are not particularly aware of the difficulty experienced by those upon whose shoulders they stand. Many teachers who came before them had to blaze a rather harsh trail so that current teachers can enjoy a better relationship with the management teams that have learned how to deal a bit more laterally with them instead of treating them strictly in that infamous vertical authoritarian manner.

When it comes to East Asian or other factory workers in Korea, they are often still quite harshly treated in a way that no one from the west would ever be able or willing to endure. Most Western foreigners are not aware of that situation either.

Working Together on Olympics Preparedness

Gangneung Westerners normally do not function outside of either an informal social setting, or an educational oversight team. Non educational management teams in the Olympic cities have had nearly no experience with foreigners either. They have not had the 30 or 40 years working together in order to learn and adjust. Hopefully, the upcoming Olympics will provide some opportunity for Gangneung and Pyeongchang to experience more projects that require Koreans and foreigners to actually work together rather than just to talk.

CHINESE / KOREAN RELATIONS

Chinese and Koreans have quite a warm affinity between their populations. Chinese especially love Korean people, and welcome them like rock stars when they visit China. This accounts for the fact that there are more Chinese immigrants to Korea than there are any other nationality of people. Chinese tourists make up a whopping 35 – 40% of all visitors to Korea as well.

China's Amazing Achievement Leaves Out More Than it Includes

Chinese people who actually live for a time in Korea don't usually want to return home. It may be true that China has raised 20 – 30 million people out of poverty during the past 20 to 30 years, but there are the other 950million rural Chinese to consider as well. And some of the dictatorial rulership factors in China are uncomfortable for the people too.

Korean Popular Culture

One reason Chinese like Korea so well is because of the popular culture. K-pop, movies, serial TV, the fashion brands, and more, are just culturally attractive to younger Chinese. But there may be more to the phenomenon.

A Common Dislike – Japan

A common dislike toward Japan is something that both cultures share. We think of world war two era Japanese atrocities, and my grandfather would have agreed. *(He was a survivor of the Bataan Death March and hated Japanese people for the rest of his life.)* My wife is Korean, and her father fought for the Japanese as a compulsory Japanese soldier during WW2, as did many other Korean men. He was actually at Hiroshima when the US dropped the bomb. He survived by spending a few days submerged in a river waiting out the fire storm. The memory of that domination by Japan is still raw in the hearts of many Korean families.

But the Chinese have no love for Japan either. My wife's Korean nephew lived in China for a few years. He sent back pictures of war museums which depict life sized statuary scenarios of Japanese laboratories. The Japanese scientists tortured, dissected, and otherwise inhumanely ravaged Chinese subjects in horrible experiments. These museums help to keep the memory, hatred and pain alive.

But the Chinese and Korean distaste for Japanese is multigenerational. Japan invaded both countries repeatedly in the pre-modern era. There is still a common feeling of angst in both countries against Japan.

Modern and Ancient Respect

China is like a father to Korea culturally, philosophically, and genetically. There are so many subtle points of commonality. But Korea is like a capitalist big brother to the Chinese, having become an economic superpower in the modern world. They both look to each other in a kind of respect for these reasons. Even with the communist / capitalist tension, among people that still look historically backwards for their primary identity, Confucius, Leo Tau, and the ancient Chinese Sage Kings are dominantly common points of heritage.

Positively Evaluating the Past

The West tends to look at our history and see periods of progressive brightness amid a mostly dark, stagnant, and backward 5,000 year history. We often tend to emphasizes more the differences than any common points between us. Asians view the past quite differently together. The wisdom of the past still trumps any bright flashes of modern history, which admittedly has only a couple hundred years track record.

WHY IS IT SO HARD TO BLEND WITH KOREANS AS A FOREIGNER?

After living in Korea for more than 8 years, I do agree that there is a more shallow language related reason why Korean people often feel uncomfortable dealing with non-natives, and that most individual Koreans have a total deficit regarding intercultural or multicultural experience. But I also have found that there is much more to the blending resistance, and it runs pretty deeply.

Korea has quite a militaristic background, conservative not progressive, and the social structure is pretty backward facing and authoritarian in nature. There is a common understanding between Korean people regarding both social order and social behavior. Non-Koreans do not fit into the order, nor do we behave in expected ways. Being from a mono-culture (I would go as far as to call it an iso-culture), the conceptual apparatus necessary for Korean people to accept other differently structured manners and ways is not readily available to their awareness.

The standard Confucian way of dealing with non-conforming social operators is to ostracize them and punish them socially so that they will change to conform, or else be marginalized. They do this to each other without even really recognizing that they do it, and it automatically kicks in toward outsiders in manifestations that are likewise subconscious and largely reflexive. The problem for Korean people is that, where-as other Koreans just accept that treatment and suffer in silence, Westerner's reactions shock and surprise Koreans. It might be like looking in a "foreigner mirror" and seeing yourself negatively through our eyes, at least in that aspect of the culture.

Even for those of us (non-Koreans) who have been here long enough to understand the behavior, we certainly don't accept it when it is directed our way, and we usually try to react in ways that will help our Korean neighbors to adapt to non-Korean situations. But doing that is not comfortable for anyone in the room.

The truth is that it will take a lot more inter-cultural exposure along with a few decades of awkward interactions in order to effect much change. And Korean people will need to learn to switch between their iso-culture standards, and inter-cultural ways more fluently than they currently do. In the meantime, there are aspects of socialization that will be uncomfortable for both sides.

UNIVERSAL HUMAN RIGHTS AND THE WOMEN'S QUESTION IN KOREA

European intellectual history shows the partiality that the male half of the human race has traditionally carried against the female half. Early on, European conservatives for example, wanted to restrict rights to privileged social elites, with the exclusion of women. At the same time, socialist thinkers wanted to extend favor to the workers, but still excluded women. Nationalists emphasized the rights of national sovereignty and national independence, but didn't look at extension of other rights to particular groups within nations. Liberals wanted to ensure equal legal rights in civil and political life, but didn't include women. In all of these early debates, women were systematically excluded on some interesting, commonly reasoned grounds.

Feminism's Theoretical Base

Feminism developed to answer this lapse. Theoretical grounds were developed in answer to the arguments against female inclusion in advancing human rights. Early on, there were some prominent arguments for women's exclusion from participation in a man's world. Early feminists had to craft arguments against them, and feminists had their own differing focus areas where they sought inclusion.

In Korea, it seems that women's movements follow modern trends, sometimes without consideration of the reason based battles that were fought to establish modern views of women in the West. Olympe de Gouges and Marry Walstonecraft were among an early generation of activists and writers who fought, and sometimes died, to establish and defend women's rights. It might be helpful for Korean people to consider those points of argument, and why the women's side won out reasonably in the West.

Feminism developed different strands early on. There was a political version, a cultural version, and a social version. The right to vote and participate in law making is different from the right to divorce. Expanding education to women was another divergent point of emphasis, among others.

Women are Similar to Men

What was often called "The Nature of Women" was an additional metric by which early diversifications of feminism were distinguished from one another. Some stressed that women had the same qualities as men when it came to reason, so they argued that women should have the same political rights. This argument was set against counter-arguments that women had their force of power in their pelvis, while a man's force was in the upper areas of his body, including his head. No wonder women won on that argument.

Women are Different From Men

Another contention was that women are different, not similar. Women are the nurturers in life, and it was important for women to have educational advantages in order to raise socially responsible children. This difference also makes them uniquely BETTER equipped to sensitively structure and manage some aspects of modern governance.

Some men claimed that women were rendered incapable of coherent social interaction for a significant portion of every month due to reproductive cycles. But women argued that these circumstances were not disqualifying frailties. What was the true frailty of women was that they had always been denied opportunities in education and social participation. Remove these disadvantages, and regardless of physical particularities, women would rise to sit respectably beside their male counterparts and contribute just as meaningfully in public life.

The most powerful impediment to women's progress in acquiring rights was the simple, stubborn position that men had always dominated, and that must be for a good reason. Religion supported men in this role, and so did other traditional institutions. But the problem for liberal thinkers was that this was the same argument that Monarchs used to support their unfair dominance over the populations. So use of this against women weakened at the same time as it weakened against representational and parliamentary forms of government.

It's Not Just A Trend – There are Reasons

Korea is adopting modern views toward women's rights quickly, but maybe without understanding well some of the blood that was spilled, and the finer points around decades of heated reasoning that underpins these modern, Western views. There were many points of logic and reason that won out at high cost over illogical, traditional views. Knowing those reasons and the price at which they triumphed may add some stability and power to the changes in attitude toward women that are going on apace here in this society.

Some foreigners claim that changes should not be made to Korean culture. Ask the women here though, if they want to go backwards, or to continue moving forward. I don't think the answer will surprise anyone who is being honest about it.

THE KOREAN SWITCH – ALTERNATING BETWEEN DIFFERENT WORLDS

There is a group of companies is Seoul that gathers for conferences together on inter-cultural cooperation. Their focus is on the ability of Korean management to interface with teams that are not Korean. This weekend, members of 7 different companies met for a series of workshops, and to rehearse some presentations for an upcoming private event on the same subject.

One on One Sessions

One aspect of my role as a consultant is to have private sessions with young Korean men who have to switch between working in a totally Korean environment, to working completely with Western, or multi-cultural teams. Using a fictitious name, let me give a brief overview of a session I had this weekend.

A young operations manager named JaeUk is in his late twenties. He is feeling stress, but he can't talk to anyone on his team because there are propriety issues with disclosure of his feelings inside the company. But as I am an outsider, he feels ok talking to me. I have played this role on occasion, and the story JaeUk tells is not unique for a young Korean manager in his position.

The Off Position – All Korean Team

He has been working within a strictly Korean company for the past 4 years, and tells me how difficult it has been for him to adjust to his new, intercultural role. In the first place, since he is among the younger members of his company, he has always been told what to do. When he receives an assignment, it always comes with a net of micro-management strings attached because the older colleagues tell him how to do it, and when to do it, but seldom why to do it that way.

That never bothered JaeUk before, because this is quite normal in his world. Things don't always go correctly, because sometimes there are too many cooks, and the right hand doesn't always know what the left is doing (*to mix metaphors*). When setbacks and failures occur, he takes the heat (*being a younger member means being a scapegoat*) , but that is just part of the landscape of Korean teamwork. He says that never really bothered him before.

The On Position – Multicultural Team

But then began the inter-cultural work, and things have changed. After working for three months with a completely Western team, he had to then come back home and try to get going again in Korea. Here is what he experienced.

First of all, upon joining the multicultural team, he felt an incredible amount of stress because there was no one to tell him exactly what to do. At first he would ask an older team member what he should do about an assignment, and they told him do it however he wanted. It completely crippled him for the first week or so. He was so nervous that he couldn't sleep and had migraines and stomach aches. But after a couple of week he started to acclimatize and learn to take initiative. He began to trust his own judgment. When he made mistakes, it was shocking to find that the other guys laughed about it, and then proceeded to help him get it straightened out.

Switching Back Off Again

Gradually, he got used to the different way of doing things, and really began to feel part of the team. But then, he had to go back to his old role. Now, a week back in, he is experiencing a new problem. It seems that his old team has noticed some changes in JaeUk. They feel that he is no longer respectful toward them, and that he has gotten proud and big headed. He takes liberties and functions outside of his correct boundaries, stepping on the toes of his older workmates.

JaeUk is feeling quite discouraged at this point, but talking about it has taken some of the load off his mind. My counsel was to apologize a lot and continue to reacclimate to his old role. I told him that he is finding his "SWITCH", and it will work more fluently after he uses it a couple of times.

We discussed more about exactly what had been happening to him, and he clearly recognizes what is going on. We both decided that he has learned valuable lessons from the experience that will make him a more valuable asset to any company he works for, in Korea or abroad.

THE KOREAN SWITCH – PART 2

This past weekend, I was at an intercultural business meeting, and yesterday, I wrote an article about a Korean manager, and his experience switching between an open Western and closed Korean management experience. This article relates the feelings and experience of a Western manager trying to work under a Korean team.

The group of organizations that I work with have a multiple of different situations, and among my roles, I do individual counseling on the operational level. I explained this a bit in part 1 of this series. I had time to talk with two foreigners at this meeting, and will start by saying how much harder it is for a foreigner to work here than it is for a Korean to work in an open situation.

Using a fictitious name, I will describe some of the experiences and feelings that "Jim" expressed in our meeting.

Frist of all, Jim is from New York, and has worked with Korean people in the overseas office of his company. He likes Korea generally; the society and the culture. He didn't expect to feel the level of frustration that he has experienced since moving here two months ago, and is teetering on the edge of giving up and going home.

He told me he has developed a feeling of "seething rage" when he deals with some members of his Korean management team. Early on, he tried to talk to his managers when there was friction, but he quickly found out that talking didn't help. Actually, trying to communicate has only made things worse. He feels that two of his Korean managers view communication as a challenge to their authority, and fight back in underhanded, political way within the social relationships inside the company. This enrages Jim, and his face turned red when he talked about it.

He described some of the underlying factors that have lead up to the current stand-off. He said that these particular managers want to put their mark on everything he does, and try to control his work so that he has no freedom and can take no satisfaction or credit from his efforts on the job. Sometimes, it is just a "Alpha Male" dominance thing, which is hard for Jim, but he can take it. Understanding the cultural inclination helps him to just bite his tongue.

But often, there is a blatant injustice involved, and this is something he can't just sit and be quiet about. There are these two particular Korean managers that he has a problem with in this area. He tried to talk with them about it reasonably, and here is what happened.

First, they denied it. But when it happened again and he approached them, they blamed him. And when he approached them about a further example in instance, they got angry and cold toward him. Then the gossip started, and what he calls "social politics" got under way. Now, he believes there is no way to fix the situation and is on the cusp of packing up to go home.

My point to him was that his situation is not unique. Others have endured worse friction in the past, and those who stick it out actually help Korean companies to learn how to deal with foreigners, and improve the situation for everyone. We also talked about how his anger might be exacerbating the situation.

He understood and even agreed. But he also shook his head, saying that he didn't think he was the right guy for the job. He feels it isn't worth it, and worries that he might explode.

THE KOREAN SWITCH – FINAL INSTALLMENT

Having shared perspectives from both sides, it's a good time for some final reflection on this article series. True, there has not been any input given from older Korean managers, but in my experience, that isn't likely to happen any time soon.

That having been said, communication is the key to integration. Both sides need to understand and make accommodations for the differences. The intent of this article is to give advice on both sides in order to help with the foreigner side of the problem.

Foreigners Need Patience and Self Control

First of all, foreigners who find themselves is a situation like Jim have to back off a bit. The situation is what it is, and it can't change instantly. It was a problem that Jim didn't know what he was getting into, so he wasn't ready for it. This caused him to react in a way that polarized the situation. Getting angry, and trying to communicate in a Western style is not the right way to go. Some pre-orientation for Jim would have gone a long way.

Koreans Do Communicate, But In a Dignified, Emotionally Controlled Manner

Korean men are not stupid, cruel, or bad. It might feel that way to a Westerner in a situation like Jim's, but not if the Westerner understands the culture. All their lives Korean males have carried the burden of expectations piled up on top of them, and they have stoically swallowed their emotions, their pride, and their words. It is honorable in their minds to do that, and they paid their dues.

We have to understand that the peacefulness and order in this society is beautiful, but not accidental. Older Koreans respect self restraint and dignity. They will listen understandingly if that respect has first been established. They are not blind to the differences, or to their need to make allowances for Westerners who are not part of their system. But there is no way they can quickly understand the differences, just as there is no way for a foreigner to deeply understand Korean culture immediately. It takes time.

Korean Responsibility – Work Hard to Understand

On the other hand, Korean managers need to understand that Westerners view themselves first as INDIVIDUALS. Suffering under an authoritarian situation is something they can't do for long. The longer they have to bite back their individuality, the more pressure will build.

A huge difference is that we have been taught all our lives to express ourselves in order to relieve stress. We have been taught to negotiate out compromises with each other, to give and take on both sides. That takes open communication.

It **does** fall upon Korean managers to try to understand. If Koreans simply remained culturally isolated and didn't invite foreigners in, there would be no need to adopt more multicultural methods. But Korean mono-culture is MONO, not multi, so it is clear that adjustments need to be made on this side of the relationship. If you are the host, you have a responsibility too. It just follows.

Mono-Cultural Methods Inadequate on Multi-Cultural Teams

The culture of Western communities has changed because it had to. It changed to accommodate more than one culture working together. The ways of the West may not be easy to accommodate, but if Korean companies want to work with Western teams, the old ways alone won't be enough to make it happen.

If Korean management wants multi-cultural teams, they are going to have to adopt at least some multi-cultural methods of dealing with these teams. That means opening up to communication, understanding, and at least some inevitable, difficult change.

FREEDOM AND EQUALITY – EAST MEETS WEST

Who is it that has true freedom in a modern society. The answer to that question depends on how one defines freedom. It also depends on which society you are evaluating.

In 19th century Western thought, social philosophers like Alexis deTocqueville and John Stewart Mill delineated more closely the relationship between equality and freedom. Since the French Revolution, the slogan "Liberty, Equality, Fraternity" had become more than just a marketing phrase for the export of French republican political liberty.

Changing Relationships – Changing World

The old feudal system of Kings, Barons and peasants was transforming into a new political world where land owners moved to scientific farming and displaced the peasant populations, who flocked to the new industrial cities to work in a different kind of slavery.

They suffered inhuman conditions while a few slick industrial magnates raked in massive mountains of cash. A new kind of 'Social Darwinian' inequality was being defined.

Revolution For Equality and Liberty

What deTocqueville and Mill discerned was that there is a certain level of equality needed in order to have any meaningful measure of liberty. This had been the driving force behind contemporary revolution. Marx seized upon that side of the issue too, in framing out his call to the workers to rise up in revolt.

But deTocqueville saw another side to the problem. His family was from the aristocratic tradition in France. His grandfather had been the lawyer for King Louis the Sixteenth (*on the losing side*), and had been executed in the terror during the 1790s. After Napoleon fell from power and the Bourbons were brought back in, deTocqueville's family had come back into favor, only to be disappointed again when the Liberal 'July Monarchy' was launched in the 1830s. The old aristocracy was displaced once again.

deTocqueville initially thought that republicanism would ultimately fail, but then he visited America and changed his mind. There, this new experiment was stable and working. But deToqueville saw another problem.

Tyranny of the Majority

His family's experience in France pointed toward what became known as "The Tyranny of the Majority". The terror during the revolution was interpreted to mean that tyranny could come from below as well as from above. This represented another challenge to individual liberty. The mob actions during the Jacobin control of the nation seemed to highlight that. Other events in history, like the European peasant wars still in recent memory, pointed to that potentiality as well. But deToquville saw it in America too, in a different way.

The program toward equality in America was squeezing out the exceptional person. Individual freedom was being amalgamated and flattened by powerful state sponsored nation building programs, by the new culture industries, and by the new emphasis on money making. There was less and less room for individuals to make any stand at all. They all thought the same, believed the same, and behaved the same. deTocqueville saw this as "The Tyranny of the Majority" in a cloaked, perhaps more sinister form.

However we evaluate the European historical process and the ideas of the new liberals, it is not hard to see their point. Without some measure of equality, there can be no liberty. But _too much_ equality starts to limit individual liberty as well.

Koreans Adopt Western Values Differently

Living in Korea, one discerns a very differently organized society that can be analyzed through the prism that Mill and deTocqueville put in place. The Confucian strict authority scenario is similar in a way to the old aristocracy. But it is different in many ways too. The changes that happened in Europe and America are different than the changes that are happening here. They started differently, and they are morphing differently. But there are many modes of comparison at the same time.

The old established male dominance in Europe, and the traditional class structure in Europe was different than the old ways in Korea. The new structures there are not the same as the new arrangements here. But the basic principles that Mill and deTocqueville laid out are still applicable.

The balance of equality in social relations will at some point either facilitate or dampen the expression of personal, individual liberty. Liberty and Equality balance in relation to each other, and the sweet spot is not a clean black line. There are no well defined parameters to mark out the optimal adjustment points, and there are just so many hard to turn dials.

Korean's View of Individual Freedom

At the same time, Koreans value liberty and equality in a completely different way than we do in the West. Traditionally, they have demoted those values way down on the list, favoring conformity, standardization, and uniformity over the individual by almost all measures.

It seems to me that in the rush to adopt Western customs and ways, Koreans would do well to school up on the deep debates and analysis of the change process that occurred in Europe and America. It would help us all to better understand and navigate the strange confluence that we experience in every day modern Korean life.

One way that I run smack into this issue is when I deal with young Korean students whose parents do not teach them the "Elder Respect" that is still so dominant in the value systems of their grandparents. The individualism of the younger generation Koreans is diametric. That change creates lonely, neglected elder generations. Can we discern the balance function between equality and liberty in situations like this? In my opinion, just a little thinking in that direction yields a lot of insight.

WHY DOESN'T KOREA HAVE ANYTHING LIKE HOME DEPOT?

Korea has hardware stores with an amazing amount of products, but they are few and far between, and not centralized or franchised like they are in the USA. And I have never seen one in a large building with a huge parking-lot, so the big ones are not really easy to find. I did some construction work for my wife's family near Wonju, and there is a pretty amazing place there with a limited selection of almost everything you can think of in the way of construction materials, but it is owned and operated by one guy. The place is organized after a fashion, but there would be no way to find anything without his personal assistance. It is incredibly cluttered and you have to walk through the place sideways because it is so crammed with stuff.

I know there are other places like that, but they are not frequented by the general public. Korean people generally do not get into home improvement projects, and even professional contractors are not really the 'do-it-all' kind of people. The entire

Korean mindset is more specialization oriented. If someone does screen repair for homes for example, that is pretty much all they do, so there are suppliers that cater just to them. That example seems to hold true in most other trades as well.

I was looking for some specialty concrete material one time and got initially excited when I found a Sika dealer. Sika is a massive company with probably over 1,000 skews covering any concrete product you can think of. But when I talked to the store owner, he only had knowledge of 5 or 6 products in a narrow area of his personal specialization. What is curious to me is that he had absolutely no interest in the industry, the technology, or in any related fields.

The point is that the Korean focus generally is narrowed into really tight areas both personally and professionally, so it seems that a supplier model based on specialization works better than a one stop shop for all related items. More could be said about the cultural implications of that trait, but that is perhaps outside the scope of this question.

KOREAN BEAUTY OBSESSION – AN AMERICAN MAN'S PERSPECTIVE

I've been married to a beautiful Korean woman for going on 23 years. She married me in the US, and we spent 16 happy years there before moving here in 2009.

My wife spends an average of 10 or 15 minutes to get ready when we go out. (Maybe 20 if it's a more formal outing). But I've seen some women who can't go out unless they first spend some 2 hours or more in their beauty ritual. From both a practical and a psychological perspective, I find this interesting.

Men Like Beauty

I realize that the cosmetics industry grooms social groups to get started on their products and get hooked. And I also realize that there is a natural and balanced desire by women to ornament themselves. As a man, of course I appreciate beauty and beautification as well. But I have to say, I really think the whole thing has gotten way out of hand.

The Cost / Benefit Measure

I reasoned with my wife about it early in our marriage, and on a few different points. First of all there is the cost

/ benefit metric. I think that the first ten minutes in front of the mirror are where a woman gets the biggest benefit from her facial artistry. After that there is a diminishing return on the time spent.

Natural VS Chemical Moisturizing

My wife, not being overly vain, had another reason why make-up and lotions are important. The eye creams seem to be some of the more expensive items (*I admit having been shocked about it the first time*), and the reasoning behind their use is to prevent wrinkles through moisturizing the delicate skin. But as a counter theory, I reasoned that the skin's natural oils are much better for moisturizing than some chemical concoction could ever be.

When my wife first stopped using eye cream however, her skin initially got drier, so she challenged my theory at that point. I told her to wait though, because using the artificial moisturizers had inhibited her skin's glandular processes, and it would take a couple weeks for them to get going again. Sure enough, 20 years later, she has wonderful, naturally soft skin (*I love it when I'm right*).

The Psychology of Naval Gazing

I also have observed a lot of competition these days between women in general. Of course, this is a sweeping generality and can't be applied on a case by case basis, but women certainly compare themselves to each other on a lot of different levels. I suppose it can be healthy sometimes, but my opinion is that it usually is not.

I have to wonder if sitting in front of a mirror and appreciating ones-self in that focused way for two or three hours per day is psychologically healthy. Self appreciation is necessary for all of us to some degree, but is there too much of a good thing going on in this case?

I realize that I could take some flak from writing and article like this, but I am also curious to hear feedback. In Korea, there is certainly a hyper-phenomenon of beauty obsession, and there are so many stories of it having gone too far. I think that half the young women in the nation are not as they appear to be, and there are sensational stories of how their husbands sue them later for having 'ugly' babies (*The stories are probably not true, but they illustrate a point*).

It's Just a Bag of Bones

I don't really believe this, but I say it to counter the emphasis the other way. You can use it if you want to. It's not copyrighted. "Skin is just a bag that holds you bones together."

CULTURAL CAMARADERIE IN AN ALIEN LAND

I most often write on a less personal note. But living in Gangneung can be quite claustrophobic, and speaking into the air may be in some way therapeutic.

I don't mean to say that Gangneung is a really lonely place to live. There are definitely other like-minded foreigners here, and the Korean population is quite accommodating. My wife is my best friend, so I am lucky that way. There are also some other guys my age here, with similar interests and similar ways of seeing the world. There are actually three or four Westerners living here that I feel a more unique closeness to specifically because we are aliens. I would like them otherwise for sure. But sharing a minority status definitely adds an edge.

Truthfully, living amid a narrow community of Westerners on the edge of the world is rich in ways that being back home could not be. How many people does someone really connect with in their life? I haven't lived in America for going on a decade. But I remember seldom having more than 3 or 4 people at any given time that I really considered to be my friends. I have the same thing here, even more.

There is something about being a minority. It seems like it should facilitate relatability. I certainly observed that among minorities back home. There was a camaraderie similar to that of being a motorcycle enthusiast. Back in Seattle, it didn't matter what kind of bike you rode, when you passed another biker, he nodded at you. You shared something on a kind of visceral level. Of course that is a shallow example.

An Example of Cultural Camaraderie

A better one would involve my African American friends. I remember on many occasions, walking along with one of my Black friends, and we would be talking, enjoying our association. But whenever we passed another African American on the street, I was automatically, naturally, understandably pre-empted. They invariably honored each other with a brief moment of almost absolute recognition. I felt completely shut out of that moment, and it happened

It is weird though among strangers, how little other foreigners feel that same twinge of commonality living here. Most times, when I do the 'motorcycle nod', the other Westerner will not nod back. I find it a bit strange that, while motorcycle guys, who actually share so little in common, will acknowledge you as a shallow compatriot of sorts, other expats, with whom I share so much more in a meaningful way, are often reluctant to give that recognition even a curt nod or a smile.

Familiarity Background

There are isolation issues on other levels as well. Back home there was a background of familiarity which definitely brought a sense of comfort and security that I don't feel living here. Thinking back, I didn't realize it then, and can barely discern it even now. I am certain of it, however. It has a distinct nostalgia in my consciousness. It's like that dream that you can't exactly remember. You only know that it was sweet, and you wish you could go back to sleep and catch whatever it was once again.

I'm not complaining, really. I am just musing about how little white Westerners have in common with each other these days. Koreans definitely feel a deep sense of connectedness in which an outsider can't share. African Americans share a grippingly emotional history, and can relate to each other on a powerful level. White guys are totally shut out of that. Even motorcycle guys have something going on between them. But how did members of my cultural group become so isolationist among ourselves? It is interesting to me, especially from this perspective, sitting here on the edge of the world in Gangneung.

IS IT A GOOD IDEA FOR A FOREINGER TO ATTEND SEOUL NATIONAL UNIVERSITY?

In Korea, SNU is touted as the best university and Korean companies compete to hire SNU graduates. Worldwide, the school ranks in the top 50 and it is known as a good research institution. Going to school in Korea has its challenges, however, and it takes some getting used to for a westerner. I am fond of saying that a Korean teacher's job is to make their students cry.

Passive learning is a Korean hallmark, and asking questions or expressing opinions can easily be viewed as challenges to a teacher's authority. That takes some getting used to, and although that situation is improving over the past, it is still an underlying issue that you will run into with some Korean professors.

Another outcome of passive learning is the production of passive employees in the workplace. It is important to understand what the Korean workplace is like in order to do well in a Korean learning institution, because the school you go to will not only teach you facts, but also instill in you some traits for the work-world. Korean lower level employees are given very little autonomy and are micromanaged in all they do. At the same time, they often get blamed when middle managers, or even upper management makes mistakes. This is expected. One thing you have to learn is to suffer in silence until you rise up a few levels. Korean people are very afraid to take any responsibility or risk due to the political climate in the workplace.

I am not saying here that this is bad, it is just different, and hard for westerners. But some of the employee traits you will learn in a Korean institution will make it hard for you to be valued in a western work environment if you proceed blithely unaware. As long as you know which 'groomings' to protect against, you can prevent Borg assimilation (an allusion to Star Trek Borg).

On the other hand, many Korean work attitudes will make you a valued member of any company. Obedience, machinelike work ethic, respect for your superiors, etc..., are all qualities that any employer will appreciate. Just be careful that you retain enough initiative after the indoctrination so that you can find your way out of a closet without waiting for direct instruction from a superior.

Korean school will probably be harder than a western school. The pace at which you have to learn is accelerated, and the amount of material you have to memorize will be double. The teaching style is different, and our western learning style is different from Korean students as well. It will take some adjustment to make it work. It will demand more from you and you will benefit in some ways. But if you plan to go back to a western country after school, just remember that what a Korean employer values in an employee is very different than what a western employer will value, and instilling those soft skills is another task that the university takes on over and above just academic learning.

THE KOREAN GENERATION GAP

Kids these days do not fit any of the old Korean norms. While generation gaps exist in every country, in Korea, the situation seems extreme. There are huge differences between grandparents and parents, and how they view the world. Then, there is another gap between parents and children.

Grandparents Have Witnessed Tremendous Change

Grandparents in Korea have the memory of post Korean war era, when there was not enough food, and absolutely no influence from the West. Their formative years infused into them a certain thousand year old set of values that doesn't really mesh well with the advancement along Western lines. But they have lived a life of radical change. I guess the same could be said of all elderly people in the world, but in Korea, where there has been huge moves from an alien eastern stance, the changes have been much faster than in most places we Westerners are familiar with.

Grandparents taught their children the strict Confusion ideals, and they were expected to control their feelings, give deep respect to their elders, and basically shrink whenever they were around adults. While the parent generation is still effected by this training, they do not extend that strict training to their kids.Only shadows of it remain, but the grandparents seem to understand.

The Entitlement Attitude

Korean kids today are absolutely privileged, at least the children that I have spent time with. They are reaping the benefits of the strict control that the older generation imposed upon itself. They don't usually show much deep respect to their elders, even though they are sweet and mostly well behaved. Some are spoiled brats, like kids anywhere, but most are pretty good kids. But although there is still a form of old Korea attitudes shown toward adults outside the family, children often treat their parents and grandparents with an entitlement attitude that doesn't bode well.

Korean mothers are so overprotective, and the kids have a completely myopic experience tunnel. The academic focus here is over the top, and the only expectation on a child is to do well in school. Many kids can't make their own beds, cook Ramen, Clean their rooms, or wash their own dishes. The way they treat their parents is often embarrassing for me to see. I know that I could NEVER have gotten away with those levels of disrespect and expectation. My parents set boundaries in those areas for sure.

I would have expected Korean grandparents to go ballistic over this situation, but the grandparents I have seen are remarkably genteel about it all. And I guess it is ok for Korean kids to grow up feeling as though they are princes and princesses, because their parents are wealthy by Western standards. This is an interesting situation in Korea too. Let me wrap up the article by describing it.

Deeply Funded Families

The relationship with the US over the past 50 years has yielded big financially to the population here. It is one of the richest per capita in the world. The nation has become an economic superpower partly from favored status with the West, but largely because of the work ethic, militaristic regimentation, and frugality of the culture. Now, many kids have no worries about money. Where-as American families go into debt, Korean families have traditionally saved money, especially the grandparent's generation. So families here are deeply funded, and that gives a lot of cushion to the younger generation. Who knows how long that will last without some crisis.

Koreans are beautiful people. The society is still a Mecca of order, peace and love. Changes are afoot, however. I hope they retain their sweetness moving forward. I guess only time will tell,

WHAT HISTORICAL CONTRIBUTORS ARE THERE TOWARD RACIAL AND CUTURAL SUPERIORITY IN THE MODERN WORLD?

Generally speaking, whenever people share a lot in common, they clump up together if exposed to outsiders. At the same time, this commonality is also a matter of context in that, when left to themselves, they focus on differences rather on commonality and end up nagging, irritating, and gossiping about each other. Social engineers understand this, and work at the macro level to give people attitudes, perspectives, and focal points that both hold them together, and provide harmless targets for the propensity to protest and grumble.

Historically, the things any 'one people' had in common were really very local in nature. Most communities were illiterate and didn't travel. Their exposure to any foreign influence was minimal or non-existent until the growth of cities resulting from the industrial revolution. Prior to that, most were peasants who lived on farms generationally, in Europe anyway, and who worked half days and half years. They were not highly motivated to do much other than scratching out enough food for the winter, for the land owners, and scratching their butts. With the advent of scientific farming, land owners in Europe were able to get 10 times the yield and began kicking their peasants off the land. Fortunately (or unfortunately according to Marx), the new industrial cities were able to hire them, and all cities began to grow exponentially throughout first part of the 1800s. The science of social engineering came into its own during this time.

With the growth of cities the culture industry was born, and it became a tool of the nation builders; local, regional, and national governments who had to find ways of making the masses malleable and controllable in their hands. Newspapers were born, telling people the common news of the nation today. Intellectuals were hired by states and employed at modern universities in order to codify common histories and create mythical national heroes that would breed a passionate commonality and patriotism in the hearts of the people. The awareness of common people grew up from their placid patches of lazy farms to encompass an informed over-arching awareness of larger maps and sister cities. Small time local family feuds were traded in on national and international rivalries. Language was codified and standardized so dialects began to disappear and socially, culturally, educationally, and informationally, we began to define ourselves with paradigms of wider sweeping, more inclusive, and more grandiose scope.

At the same time, the ideology of rule by the people was advanced, and civic responsibility began to take on new meaning. The king was no longer an agent of God, or a god himself, but an employee of the people, and ostensibly hirable or firable by their will. Legitimacy of power is claimed now to come through a kind of social contract, and citizens supposedly share a common charge both in the rule and defense of the nation.

Modern nationalism and patriotism creates an ethos of hyper-superiority and can morph, especially in times of war, into a very ugly and in-humane business. Also, it tends to linger generationally after the war is over. Often, families of those currently in the military, those who have served before, and those whose have families that have sacrificed their lives in service of the country tend to comfort themselves with feelings of passionate, even religious justification for the horrors they have lived through. Many religions along with secular agents of the nation egg on this kind of perspective, although not everyone buys into it.

Finally, there is the pinnacle of the progressive trajectory that began during the colonial times and endures to this day. I feel it myself as a westerner with a conscious measure of chagrin. The fact that it was white Europeans who launched and presided over the scientific revolution, and that for thousands of years more quaint and static cultures made little or no progress, presents a seductive justification for the prejudicial mindset described as the white man's burden. I don't like that in myself and try to fight it. But the world is full of the productions and benefits of western science, and although it is ok to be proud of that, I guess, we should beware the slippery slope that attends.

A GRANDFATHER'S LIFE – GANGNEUNG STORY

Near Gangneung there lives a elderly grandfather (halabogee) whose life spans the Korean war. He lived under the Japanese occupation of Korea, and shared his memories with me one afternoon, sitting on the porch of his house. His only child was adopted, and now lives nearby. But his wife passed away quite a number of years ago. Now, he lives alone.

Pencil Nubs

We sat there on his porch and he told us of what it was like to be a young boy going to a school run by the Japanese. He said that they didn't have pencils, so many students had to share one pencil stub that had been ground down to a mere nub. Even so, if the schoolwork was not done the next day, the consequences were grievous.

Cardboard Shoes

It was impossible to get shoes back then. He had to make new shoes for himself every day. He described to me how he would cut cardboard pieces for the sole, and how to create a rough twine out of straw, or dried grass. This way, he could lash his cardboard shoes onto his feet with the twine and usually get through a day before they fell apart.

Winters were unbearable. The schools had no heating, and the students had inadequate clothes. Many children suffered serious frostbite, and some were crippled by it for life.

He didn't want to talk about the war. But he did speak of later periods of his life, when he was able to get credentials as a mechanical engineer. This way, he could support his wife and adopted son until he retired as quite a wealthy man.

A Kind and Peaceful Heart

The kind, gentle grandfather spoke with peace and happiness about his life. He is in his mid 80s now. Recently, one of his grandsons was married. His daughter in law mentioned to him one time that her son needed an apartment. That was all she needed to say, because he immediately went to the bank and withdrew 6 figures.

CHINESE EXCHANGE STUDENT ANALYSIS

Some time has passed since the Exchange Student program between Chinese and Korean students concluded. iExperienceKorea has taken time to question some of the Korean parents and students about the outcome. At least one interesting comparison has become clear. This article compares the level of individuality that Korean and Chinese kids feel.

Compared to Chinese kids, individuality seems to have grown up a bit differently here. At the same time, the generation from which Korean parents come recognizes the Chinese children's attitudes in this regard. Korean parents can still relate to the Chinese kids in interesting ways.

Korean Kids – Informal and Carefree

In Korea, we witnessed the uniformity differential when watching the Chinese kids together with the Koreans. The Chinese wore uniforms, followed stricter protocol for being polite and interacting with others, and were more stiff and practiced. They seemed less relaxed, more serious performing public speeches. There was a noticeable difference in formality and carefulness among the Chinese students.

The Korean kids, on the other hand, were more relaxed and joyful in their overall demeanor. They were less concerned with making a good show, and they displayed their true feelings much more freely. When they were unhappy, they showed it. When they were pleased, they acted that way. They were noticeably less reserved and less inhibited in these ways than the Chinese children were.

Parents Relate to Both Worlds

People from the older generations in Korea understood how the Chinese kids acted. One Korean who grew up in that earlier era explained that her parents had taught her how to control the display of any free emotions. The idea was that she was not the only, nor the most important person in the room. This meant that she had to maintain an even mood so as to not call undue, inordinate attention to herself in relation to others who were present.

Some Lack of Understanding Between the Kids?

Some of the Korean kids felt that their Chinese counterparts changed their attitudes toward them a little bit negatively during the stay in China. After analyzing the dynamics, it may be that a lack of respect was being displayed toward the Korean youth due to the differences described above. If the Chinese students felt that the Korean kids were behaving with some lack of strict emotional self control, it would explain the change in attitude once they returned to their homes in China.

Individuality – The Newly Accepted Norm

The relaxing of social expectations has a positive result in many ways for Korean kids when compared to the strictness of generations past. Fewer expectations means more freedom. I just think of how the middle generation younger Korean women always have to serve the family when Koreans get together for holiday meals. It is quite a burden on these younger ones, but that expectation is changing. It is hard to imagine the same kind of demands being placed on the youth of today's generation.

This is just another example of the richness of the Korean experience in a time of rapid adjustment. The old ways exist in some measure of harmony with radically new ways of doing and seeing things. Once again, it seems that love is the lubricant that keeps everyone smiling as these changes go on apace.

WHAT IS IT LIKE TO WORK IN SEOUL?

Living in Seoul as a foreigner is great for the first couple of years. Korean people are highly hospitable and generous as a rule, and are able to have a good time. And they are normally very kind. The city itself is ultra modern and has a vibrant night life, if you are into that sort of thing. I'm getting old now and don't party as much, but Koreans like to spend social time together and aren't shy about partying.

There is a kind of surface level where all is good, but it is hard to gain any real deeper traction here as a foreigner. Korean society is pretty exclusive, and in many ways it creates a kind of pseudo anonymity that is seductive and pleasant at first. There are not many social expectations placed on foreigners, and that is kind of nice initially because you live on the edge of society in a liberating bubble of light personal responsibility. After a while though, I think healthy people begin to realize that they would like to try to be a bit more relevant, and this is where some discomfort can develop over time. Of course, that too is a matter of personality and personal maturity as well.

It is not that Korean people don't want to interact in deeper ways with foreigners, but they just don't have well developed mechanisms to do so. Koreans are not individualists like westerners are. Koreans are collectivist in nature, and all of their behaviors are nested within concentric penopticonic (allusion to Jeremy Bentham) over-layers of social politics that we simply do not have the cultural capital to meaningfully engage. Not only are we not equipped to deal with that, it would drive us insane even to try.

For this reason, more than 50% of Korean managed foreign employees still go rogue and self destruct in the short term. Foreigner employee attrition is pretty high even now, after decades of integration experiments within corporations. Some companies have figured out that managing westerners is completely different than managing Koreans, and if you get into a company that has some sophistication that way, it can be really good. But if you get caught in Korean office politics, it will crush you and likely spit you out like a watermelon seed.

If you can find a balance and a comfort in that situation, I think you would be really enriched by taking the job and experiencing Korea in that intimate way. I have been here for almost 9 years now and really love it, although I still have a hard time with the social politics and the limitations imposed on me by what I described above. I love Korean people and ways and you probably would too. All in all, I highly recommend Korea, at least for a couple of years, maybe more, depending on how you are doing then.

STAYING POSITIVE IN A KOREAN WORK ENVIRONMENT

More than anything else for a Westerner, dealing with the management structure in Korea is difficult. In the West, our relationship with managers in an office setting is more relaxed, but in Korea it is blisteringly rigid and it chaffs. That is not to say there are no politics or no power moves in a Western company. There certainly are. But what happens in Korea is by far, a harsh alien world in comparison.

Although Korean systems of management don't work with Westerners, it can be said that Western styles don't work well with Koreans either. If the team is mostly made up of Koreans, and if Koreans are the older, titled members of the staff, there is little chance at this point in time of shifting to a more open style of authority expression.

If you are a Western operator in a Korean system, here are a few things to think about. They might help.

1. First of all, it is easy to get negative, but it is important to resist that trend. Being away from one's own culture, and having to stomp one's ego down every day to fit into a strict, military style structure, isn't easy. It can quickly

wear one down. The best thing to do is focus on being helpful and accommodating, and to just give up any feelings of ownership in your job. People will step on you unfairly and it can't be helped. But if you are close to your lower level Korean team members, you will see that it is much worse for them, although they are accustom to it. Staying positive and helpful to the people around you is the best medicine while you adjust to other discomforts.

2. Secondly, remember that Koreans are looking for humility, respectability, and dependability. If you defer to the leader, he will usually relax. If you don't it will get worse. Regarding respectability, don't have any emotional outbursts AT ALL. Keeping your cool is something that Koreans teach their middle school kids, and they will view you as an elementary child if you show your frustrations. Finally, dependability is where you always do your part, no matter what. Do these three things, and you will eventually make a place in the organization, hands down.

3. Try to remember that if you can make it work, it will be a powerful notch in your belt. Not only will other companies recognize your skill and respect you, but you will naturally gain deeper qualities within yourself. These

good traits will help you in all your relationships, and in anything you do.

4. Other than that, try to learn the language and make personal friends. The insight you get from seeing Korean people with their families will make you love them, because it is an beautiful culture made up of beautiful people. If you love something, you can put up with a lot more for it.

THE RIO GAMES COMPARED TO KOREA

Most of us are aware by now that the Olympics in Rio are under the curse of bad news. Whether it turns out to be fair or not, an interesting question comes out of it. How does Korea compare? Will similar problems be a concern of the 2018 Winter Olympics here? Let's look at that question on a few counts.

Disease Control

Zika virus is a disease issue that is hovering over the Rio games. How would Korea rate in managing a situation like that? Well, just last year there was a test with MERS. How did the disease control authorities, the hospitals, and law enforcement perform? After some criticism (*maybe unfair*) for being slow to respond, the government here absolutely cracked down on the problem. The resources and organization employed was exemplary and effective.

Safety in Rio is a big concern for athletes and visiting fans. Paralympics competitor, Liels Tesch of Australia was robbed by crooks. Another non Olympic athlete from New Zealand reports being robbed by the police, who are protesting for not being paid by the city. The economy and the state of the protective services there, police and fire included, don't inspire much confidence. How does Korea compare?

Even in Seoul, crime is low. But out here in Rural Korea, a lot of people, even businesses, still leave their doors unlocked. Police get paid without fail, like a heartbeat, and are totally dedicated to their jobs. The military is at the ready, and the young soldiers even come out to help shovel snow during the heavy weather. Kids run around free, and their parents don't worry about them at all, crime-wise.

Absentee Athletes

Rio is also going to be missing quite a few of its visiting Olympics athletes. We can't really compare the doping problems Russia is having, but the reluctance of the golfers to come is related to risks. In Korea those risks are diminutive, as we have been explaining.

Pollution

Air and water pollution is another negative factor for Rio this year. In Seoul, the air pollution is admittedly a problem in the summer. But in the winter, even there the air is pleasant. There have been large regulatory efforts over the past couple of decades that have made the city much cleaner.

Water is not a problem either. Every home and office has water filtration, even though the tap water is not really a big issue. The beaches here on the East Coast are pristine. The biggest Korean Olympic City has under 250,000 residents. Although people do leave a little trash around now and then, it is quickly picked up. You can walk barefoot and roll around in the sand in bliss without fear of being infected by anything but fun.

Dead Floating Bodies

Dead bodies or body parts seem to be showing up in Rio every couple of days lately. Again, in Seoul there are the typical crimes you see in every big city, but they are minimal in comparison to most. Here though, on the isolated, ultra-conservative, pristine East Coast of Korea, occurrences like that are so seldom as to be for all practical purposes off the table.

Construction Issues

Finally, Rio has been having construction issues. Now, I am not going to say that Korean Construction is up to the standards of countries like Canada or the US. The buildings here, and the fixtures start wearing down after about 15 or 20 years.. And things that look good from a distance tend to have some issues when examined up close. but everything works well. People remodel here about every ten or 15 years, and the Olympics will be long over by then. So, no problem on that count either.

All in all, Korea will suffer no ill repute from the scrutiny they will receive from their Olympics hosting opportunity. True, that scrutiny will likely be heightened after the issues at Rio. but have no doubt about the diligence and industriousness of this small nation. Koreans have a healthy pride too, hot and hard. There is no way these kinds of issues are going to pop up here. Rest assured.

ARE KOREANS REALLY OPEN TO OTHER CULTURES?

As a rule, Korean people would really like to be open to other cultures. Actually, they really try to be that way. There are challenges to being so, however, and it takes some hard knocks usually in order to begin to define what these challenges are. There are some inhibiting attitudinal constructs in the Confucian philosophical framework that are designed to reject differences, and they are at first unconscious to Korean people, but are exposed and defined through the crucible of intercultural exposure.

Confucian social order was a deliberate design intended both to optimize and freeze social structures and norms. It works pretty well to resist tolerance toward cultural difference. In fact, this again is largely what Confucius intended it to do, and a Pollyannaish desire to tolerate quickly runs into Confucius, who is a pretty tough customer even though he has been dead for 2,500 years. Even when Korean people begin to realize this so that tolerant/intolerant behaviors can become choice for them instead of socially programmed reflex, it is still hard to really open up for a couple of reasons.

First of all, there is an aversion to addressing problems directly. The cohesion of the society allows for problems to be covered over and managed rather than solved. In some way, maybe solving problems means change, and admiting problems means admitting that society is not really optimized after all. This is anathema to strict conservatism, and that is what Confucian philosophy is all about. Cross culture interaction does create friction, which intelligent adjustments can reduce. So one has to realize what is causing the tension and do something cause and effect related about it. It isn't always as simple as just having a smile and a willingness to engage.

The other big issues, as I see it, is that Korean people have to operate within Korean society, which is very specialized. If they turn down their Korean behavior in order to be more practically open to foreign cultures, they have to be able to turn it back up again when they go back into their normal everyday lives. Developing a responsive switch is hard for them, it is a personal journey, it is often painful, it takes time, and there just isn't much opportunity to flip (practice) the switch, so it sticks.

So yes, Korean people are open minded and want to be interculurally accepting. However, there are practical impediments to their doing so, and there is the rub...

COLLECTIVE DECISION DYNAMICS – PART 1

When we make plans that involve other people, we have to predict human behavioral reactions to our idealized models. Most often, the real outcomes and responses are far from what we initially predict. The factors involved in collective decision making are radically complicated in comparison to individual decision making scenarios.

The dynamics of the differential involved in this complexity are a focus of much study as disasters increase around the globe, and as social media systems yield rich data for analysis. BNS Experiments (*Behavioral Network Science*) that focus on collective cooperation and problem solving have shown that human subjects can perform at remarkable levels collectively, both in competitive and cooperative tasks. But social interactions can also break down cooperation in specific ways that specially designed BNS Experiments can help analyze.

Social Interaction Breakdown

An example of cooperative breakdown is when social interaction randomly effects otherwise planned traffic flow. Another example is when it leads to a "mob mentality" that can result in emotionally powerful inhibitors, interrupters, or anomalous redirectors. The most extreme of these can reach the level of emotional, even physical violence. We can see the effect of these "Social Interaction Breakdowns" in social media exchanges and in the outworking of failed disaster plan scenarios. The stress and failure observed in these situations is quite prominent relative to their lower intensity and lower occurrence rates in competitive or cooperative game scenarios.

Defining Failures as Communication Based

More collectivity creates communication issues in a number of categories that can be listed. Just a few such categories follow:

1. Cultural Categories – (*Including authority structures the effect inter and extra cultural communication*)
2. Language bridges – (*including pre-preparative formalistic and technological tools*)
3. Technological Systems – (*which can increase or decrease fluidity of communication*)
4. Broadcast VS Peer to Peer Communication – (*granularity, reach, consistency, and adaptability*)
5. Temporal Urgency Based on Fixed Events in Scheduled Time – (*includes task performance,*

> *interdependency*   *failure,*   *and*
> *stress/responsibility fracture*)

iExperienceKorea is working interculturally in the area of Olympics Preparedness. As a group of Western foreigners, we have made one round of attempts to collaborate with iso-culture Korean community operatives. In this role, we have experienced different types of communication and decision making friction on the Governmental, Corporate, Media, and Community levels. This is the first of a series of short articles that will attempt to analyze first attempt cooperative outcomes from a BNS perspective. Stay tuned for more case study based analysis.

COLLECTIVE DECISION DYNAMICS – PART 2

In part one of this series, we spoke about a success / failure analysis regarding how social interactions can break down cooperation. The analysis methods of BSN (*Behavioral Network Science*) and more traditionally, Social Network Science, are useful in reviewing cooperative friction in intercultural exchange.

Social Network Science

Traditionally, social clusters have been organized in the following way:

- **Micro** – Usually refers to an individual, otherwise called and actor.
- **Dyadic** – Refers to two individuals in a relationship.
- **Triadic** – Refers to three individuals in a relationship.
- **Meso** – Refers to a population size that is large enough to generate statistical data, but small enough to prevent data overload.
- **Macro** – At this level, personal interactions are impossible to trace, so outcomes are studied.

Describing a Cooperative Failure

Earlier this year, the IEK was approached by high level Korean officials, and they asked us for help. A committee of 3 arranged a meeting, and made what appeared to be firm overtures. They specifically told us certain points of associative support that they would offer in a relationship where we provided consultation and services.

Based on these overtures, we at iExperienceKorea went to work and established points of value that fit what we understood to be the Korean committee's expressed needs.

We selected one of the three Committee Members due to his role and his English ability, and made further contact. We updated him on the action we had taken and the progress we had made. At this point, he told us that we went too fast and he withdrew, saying that the expressions his committee had made at our initial meeting were informal

iExperienceKorea had spent upwards of $8,000.00 at that point in response to their request. We were surprised. What went wrong? What misunderstandings occurred that led to this kind of cooperative failure?

Role Theory

An attendant system of analysis that attaches to Social Network Science is Role Theory. It looks like this:

1. Divisions in social groups are based on interaction protocol between heterogeneous specialized positions that we call roles.
2. In 'roles', there are permitted behavior patterns that are defined by norms that a particular society holds.
3. 'Actors', or specific individuals, are the ones who take up said roles.
4. If an individual approves of the social norms, and accepts a particular role, they will make sacrifices and incur costs to conform. They will also take measures to punish, or redirect others who act outside of the accepted social norms.
5. Changing external circumstances can change the norms, which in turn change the roles in a society. This clearly requires overcoming tradition based resistance, and is usually a difficult process.
6. Agents submit to often difficult, even humiliating roles due to their rewards / punishment expectations.

In taking a Role Theory view of how social interactions potentially inhibited cooperation between two cultural organizations, we gain multi-level insight.

Korean VS Western Social Norms

Modern Western social norms are in many ways diametrically opposite to Korean. At the dyadic level of interaction, complete disconnects can occur because of this. One person, looking the other person in the eye, can say things and be completely misunderstood.

On the triadic level, social interaction becomes much more complex. And Korean interaction becomes even more complex than Western. The expectations between Korean social operatives are first hierarchical. In the West, expectations are performance based first, and much more individual. While an operative's title, age, and support from the social framework are factors in the West, they are only small ones, where as evidence of performance success and capability are top. Korea is almost completely opposite in many respects.

In Western norms, actors can operate much more autonomously, but in Korean norms, this is not true. When a Korean actor says something, it can never really be a personal commitment due to the hierarchical nature of the norms. And due to this, Koreans often don't see either their own expressions or those of others as an immediate call to action. It is just a step in a process to get their collective to begin focusing it's hierarchical support. In other words, the dyadic level of social interaction is demoted way down in priority. It can actually frighten, maybe even threaten Korean agents to see other agents acting effectively on their own.

Defining New Norms and Roles

In closing this second installment, iExpereinceKorea can make a couple of observations that we have made before. Korean social expectations are based on a tradition that only they share among their closed culture. While it is important for outsiders to try to understand and accommodate that, outsiders are going to be not only unwilling to approve of all Korean norms, they likewise will be unwilling to accept all Korean role expectations.

But let's suspend reality for a moment and imagine a Westerner who was willing to shackle himself or herself with all the alien expectations and completely embrace all the alien roles. The reality is that in some things they could easily do so. In other things they could, but it would be hard. But in many ways, it would simply be impossible.

This purports that understanding and willingness to see different norms, and accept different roles is a bi-lateral, multi party need. Foreigners sometimes say, "You have to do things differently because you are mono-culture, and this is a multi-culture situation." This is true. But Koreans sometimes say, "You have to do things Korean style, because you are in Korea." This is also true.

So there is clearly a need for hybrid norms to be discovered, and hybrid roles to be accepted on both sides of any cooperative effort if it is going to succeed. And as point 5 in the Role Theory synopsis points out, resistance on both sides can make that a difficult process which requires repeated tries.

COLLECTIVE DECISION DYNAMICS – PART 3

In part 1 and part 2 of this series, we outlined four different metrics by which we can measure social interaction as a window into cooperative analysis. Let's just recap those so that we can see them all together.

Take the Test!

First, there was the 'Big 5' personality metric, which can be measured by honest answers to 46 different questions. You can take the test here. It will rate your personality on the big five inventory, which are as follows:

1. Extravertness – (Introvertness)
2. Agreeableness – (Disagreeableness)
3. Conscientiousness – (Irresponsibility)
4. Neuroticism – (Magnanimity)
5. Openness – (Protectiveness)

It is worthwhile, considering the cultural focus of this series, to note that individuals are not the only entities that exhibit these traits. Different cultures, as well as different organizations can be measured on this scale as well.

Communication Factors

The second metric was a four point communicative factor scale that we loaded down with truncated lingo. Let's add a little meat to those bones here in this rehash:

Communication Failure Based on Cultural Factors

We specified 'authority structures' here, and I specifically had in mind some of the communication inhibitors that arise in a hierarchical leadership environment. In Korea, leaders can easily view many important types of communication about operative inefficiencies (of *which they desperately need to know*) as authority challenges. Leaders are also often reluctant to expose themselves to the political risks inherent in open, sincere communication.

Language Bridges That Fail

Technology failures are easy to define. Google Translate, for example, does a fair job of bridging on a word by word basis, but lexical, morphological, syntactic, sematic, pragmatic, and discursive ambiguity is notoriously difficult for any tech based system to accommodate.

So we work with pre-preparative forms, and try to lean on them as translative bridges. We write them in our own language, and depend on others to translate them into the target language, hoping that nothing gets twisted around, left out, or added in the translation work. But the effectiveness of this is sometimes less than satisfactory. These tools are often crafted for a specific use, but can then taken by other operatives and used in scenarios where they maybe won't work, or could even create problems. And when failures happen around them, we can never really put our finger on exactly why it happened.

Broadcast and Peer to Peer Communication

Broadcast communications are what comes down to everyone in the system, high and low. They have to be interpreted and implemented, with detail added and enactment worked out real time. As we all know, we plan macro, but what works out micro is always fraught with surprises, adjustment, workarounds, and even complete rewrites. This is minefield of potential miscommunication.

Peer to Peer communication is what happens on and individual basis, and dyadic principles of relationship balance come into play. But both on the Broadcast and

Peer to Peer levels, politics, authority issues, language barriers, and Big 5 factors all play a complex, mixed part.

Temporal Urgency Based on Events Scheduled in Time

On projects that include the stitching together of independent tasks, problems with one task can clearly be kept secret, create stress, and potentially derail the entire schedule. A whole new level of communication sensitivity materializes. The previous sentences describe what is meant by these three definitives:

a. Task performance
b. Interdependency Failure
c. Stress/Responsibility Fracture

Social Network Science

From part 2 of this article series, we briefly outlined skeletal overviews of Social Network Science, with its dependent concept of Role Theory. Here they are in review.

Social Network Science analyzes scalingly complex relationship based on the following structure:

1. Micro
2. Dyadic

3. Triadic
4. Meso
5. Macro

Role Theory

Role Theory supposes that relationships are taken up and managed based on a broad system of contractual give and take.

1. All societies define specialized positions we call 'roles'.
2. Collectively established and policed 'norms' are defined by society. "Roles' are derived from these 'norms'.
3. 'Actors' are individuals (or collectives) who take on these roles by an act of will.
4. If an 'actor' approves and accepts 'norms' and 'roles', they will incur costs, and mete out punishments to defend them.
5. 'Roles' should change when circumstances force re-defining of the 'norms'. Since tradition resists change, sometimes 'roles' and 'norms' desynchronize. This can cause havoc and frustration.

6. 'Agents' will endure extreme difficulty holding to established 'roles' whether they are still in sync with contemporary 'norms' or not..

Having completed an inadequate review of some tools from BNS, we have to acknowledge how complex all of these factors together are. If you have played with the statistical math of combinatorcs, you know that the outcomes in an analytic system as vast as has been laid out here are practically incalculable.

Fortunately, these are all areas of perspective where we are all already expert, so we can wax intuitive over most of it, and use these 20 listed items for running prismatic insight passes over situations like the failures that iExperienceKorea suffered as described in **Part 2** of this series. Part 4, the final article, will take that up, although in extreme brief. An exhaustive analysis attempt would, of course, exhaust us.

COLLECTIVE DECISION DYNAMICS – FINAL INSTALLMENT

The last installment in this series is going to use a limited number of analysis points from our list of 20. We will explore the scenario outlined in Part 2, where IEK experienced friction in attempts to work with Korean organizations.

Our Program in a Nutshell

iExperienceKorea has a 6 member board, 5 of whom are Foreigners. I personally have relationships with a number of Korean Corporations, working with them in a consulting role. The framework of our approach is to bring Corporate dollars to specific areas of Olympics Preparedness effort here.

IEK Programs

1. Programs for Exposing local service providers to foreigner interaction and helping them to improve interaction quality.
2. Programs for creating, translating, and archiving content for educating Olympics enthusiasts about Korea's Olympics City Communities and culture.

3. Programs for attaching Corporate messaging to our growing community service based message platform to benefit them.

In order to do this, iExperienceKorea brought a Korean media (TV/radio) agency together with a Korean for profit Corporation, and we sat down with one of the Government Representatives who had asked IEK to get involved. The Corporate involvement was key here, because their funding would help fuel the programs for the service providers, and help fund the creation of the content, as well as the translation of it into multiple languages.

What Just Happened?

The dyadic phase of the effort went quite smoothly, and this allowed for the first collective meeting to be scheduled. One on one relationships with the Corporation's CEO had gone well, and one on one relations between IEK and the Media agency did also. We had all defined our roles, and were generally on the same page. But when the meeting actually took place, all those relationships fell under the spell of a Korean hierarchy dynamic.

Using a Social Network Science prism, here is what seems to have happened. There were now 4 entities in the room. I was the sole representative for the IEK, and I am a foreigner. The other three parties were all Korean. A powerful Korean pecking order came into play, and IEK, who organized and sponsored the meeting, was completely shut outside of this powerful dynamic. The oldest, highest level person was the Government official, and his viewpoint influenced all the Koreans at that meeting while he was there. Finally, at the end, he clearly stated that IEK moved too fast. Effects of his sharp withdrawal lingered even after he left.

After the official's departure, the Producer of the media company took over, ignoring IEK's needs and desires. The CEO of the Corporation had come completely prepared to invest in IEK's initiatives, but had been discouraged somewhat by the official's reticent attitude and politically protective disrespectful comments toward IEK. The media company representative then actually told the CEO that investing IEK's messaging initiatives was not a good idea.

By Korean standards, the CEO was higher on the authority meter than the Producer was, but by a Big 5 metric, the producer has a more aggressive and intense personality type. He later told me that since I was there, and had arranged the meeting, he felt the strictures of Korean protocol thrown off, and in the absence of the elderly Korean official, he felt free to let his personality rage.

In the outworking of this final result, some very specific social interactions occurred in which cooperation was inhibited. Let's close by debunking what happened.

Big 5 Cultural

Korean culture is generally less open, more neurotic, and more introverted than Western culture, and this accounts in part for the label upon IEK as "going too fast". But from a Western standpoint, saying that at a meeting IEK hosted in response ONLY to the same government's request to us for help was not very conscientious. As mentioned in part 2, Koreans fear being held responsible for things because of the collective and political nature of their decision making dynamics. But some recalcitrant behavior is damaging to others, and that comment in that context could be viewed by a Westerner as irresponsible with potentially fraudulent undertones, given the circumstances.

Big 5 Individual

At the IEK, I pushed forward with the shape and arrangement of the meeting under scrutiny here. On the Big 5 scale, I score high in agreeableness, extraversion, conscientiousness and openness. But I can tend to fret the particular details, not in a neurotic way I hope, but because I know how important some of them are. The personality impact of the Producer was the greatest, simply due to myself being largely left out of the conversation. In a triadic situation, impact imbalance is easy without equal representation, and the language barriers left the IEK under represented there.

Communicative

1. **Cultural – Authority** Clearly, the authority of the elderly governmental official tipped the entire meeting to his angle. In the West, that would not have happened. There is enough respect for personal and organizational individuality so that if one party is tentative, they would normally have been careful not to influence other parties either way. Even if they tried, the other parties would not be as influenced. Korea is different.

2. **Language Bridges** I had pre-prepared translated forms that outlined the IEK program, but they were almost completely ignored at the meeting. Even though I had dyadically gone over them in person with each participant, in the meso setting, and even in the triadic, there was basically only Korean communication, which left

me completely at sea with no rudder. None of the Korean parties respected the fact that I had called the meeting. If I had been able to keep to the forms, or to understand the swaying of the Korean dialogue, I believe that my interjections and steering efforts would have completely changed the outcome.

3. **Broadcast – Peer to Peer** The program that the IEK outlined was the Broadcast communication in this situation, and it was not respected by any of the Korean parties. Only the CEO kept quiet and kept it in mind. On the peer to peer communication, it broke down into a free for all where the pecking order defined by cultural authority and Big 5 personality factors inflicted near total breakdown of the cooperative effort.

4. **Temporal** My own efforts to do discovery, and to prepare and inform all parties was the only temporal factor to evaluate here. It was difficult to discover levels of interest and cooperative intent, and it required multiple contacts, trips, translated documents, and conversations in order to bring it together. Had I postponed the meeting to a future time, giving myself more time to get everyone on the same page, I don't think it would have made any difference in outcomes in this case. The other disruptive factors were

just too powerful for a temporal adjustment to have changed results very much, I think.

Norms and Roles

This was a situation where the Producer of the Media company, at least, expressed disorientation due to the presence of a foreigner. The other parties stuck strictly to Korean norms and roles. Since they knew instinctively that I didn't fit any of their norms, they simple passed over me, even though I was the one who brought them together.

In the case of the government official, he purposefully chose to apply strict Korean norms to his relationship with me, although he knew they didn't fit. In this case I would recommend that he explore alternative approaches if he ever really wants to cooperate with non-Korean entities in any way. New norms and role categories need to be conceived, because even if I wanted to take on his, there are many that I could not accommodate. Also, there are many that I just don't want to take on. The benefits of cooperation with him do not outweigh my distaste for some of the expectations, injustices, and indignities that would ride along with them.

Triadic – Meso

The analysis of the Micro, Dyadic, Triadic and Meso levels of Social Network have already been included in the analysis above, so they require no further exploration here.

If I were to distill a lesson down to a couple of sentences, it would be something like this. If you are a foreigner trying to build a cooperative among a group of Korean concerns, keep the effort at the dyadic level, and just do it without any collective confabs until such time that material and practical commitments have been made. Never try to go beyond the triadic level face to face at any time. And make your pre-preparative forms simple and to the point. Then stick to them religiously to prevent chaos. I believe if I had done those things differently, the first cooperative attempt would have seen much more success.

WHAT IS FORBIDDEN IN WESTERN CULTURE?

The answer to that question is morphing all the time, of course, and must include a perspective of the intellectual history of the west. This could be seated in Greek thought and in Judeo-Christian tradition, but it has also grown up from the French Enlightenment and the revolutionary upheavals both in America and in France. During that era, all the *..isms* of our time also raised their flags in western consciousness. Liberalism, feminism, romanticism, nationalism, capitalism, etc... all contribute to the values that westerners share, and these values still define our taboos and traditions in in whole and in part.

At the same time, progressivism, post modernism, and a new age ethic have been chipping away at pure rational empiricism and at classic 18th and 19th century Logical Positivism (the idea that anything science cannot describe is nonsense) as well as eroding the traditions of western religious roots. In many cases, what used to be bad is good, and what used to be good is bad. Many things that were correct in the past are incorrect now, and visa versa.

I submit therefore, that our taboos are derivative from the Judeo-Christian ethics as modified by the "isms" of the 18th century. The ten commandments would be a good place to start, but then there was liberalism.

Liberalism brought the west an emphasis on liberty and equality, so anything that challenges these values is "forbidden", or at least intensely challenged in our cultures.

Feminism relates to liberalism, because although early liberals defended the rights of most of the human race, they still excluded women from their program. So limiting a woman's rights in any way is "forbidden".

The romantic hero elevated the individual and our isolated quest for truth and meaning. People like Buddy Holly, Janice Joplin, Elvis Presley, Jimmy Hendrix and Kurt Cobain are modern day romantic heroes who died young seeking their own path. Criticizing another persons art, and inheriting wealth and privilege from outside of yourself is not really forbidden, but the self made man and the courageous individual who farts in the face of establishments expectations has become favored in our culture.

To criticize national warfare is a no no, especially during times of war. We have freeness of speech, but it is forbidden to dishonor the sacrifices that our fellow citizens have made in war in behalf of our freedoms.

Capitalism represents the American Dream, and it is forbidden to recommend communism and socialism over capitalist democracy. Or at least it has been for decades since the cold war era.

There are many more taboos that we could point too, and these few examples go to illustrate that they derive from past wrinkles in our intellectual history. Anti-polygamy sentiments derive from Judeo-Christian belief, do not steal is more universal and ubiquitous than that. Our hatred for slavery may come from something else. The point is to focus on the cause, not the effect in analyzing the causes.

Things change, and in my view the answer to this 'forbidden' question lies in a swirl of influence rather than in a codified list, because the influence perspective allows understanding and room for multiple world views, which is what we really truly have, not just one.

IS THE SHIFT TOWARD SECULARISM THE CAUSE OF INCREASED NIHILISM IN THESE CULTURES?

Religions systems are not the only belief structures that recommend seeking meaning in life, living life with some kind of purpose, and conforming to a system of humane morality. But overall, it is hard to argue against the seeming fact that religious education programs have historically been most effective in conveying these precepts out into their subject societies at large.

Modern nation states have attempted to replace systems of religious education with secular stand ins, but the subject matter of these curriculum are usually light on moral and inspirational pedagogy. In the west, materialism and nationalism have been the most salient arguments for motivating societies, and with competitive underlying foundations like capitalism and survival of the fittest, they have proven to have much less cohesive power than the traditional religious motivators had in the past.

Modern rational empiricism based on logical positivism recommends that if any precept can not be empirically confirmed, it should be relegated to the realm of nonsense, and this include morals, ethics, aesthetics, emotion, metaphysics, and religion.

Carl Sagan took the heliocentric revelation and popularized the "Copernican Principle", recommending that the Earth and its inhabitants are nothing special.

Post Modern and New Age philosophers like Derrida and Foucault have argued for a radical skepticism and moral relativity and gained huge audience in doing so.

Above are some of the influences that have contributed to the propensity toward nihilistic attitudes, but most people are looking for some way to orient otherwise for mental health issues. Nietzsche tried to be an "overman", taking the bold step out from under any established system of meaningfulness to establish his own, but he died in a mental institution. His point in defining the overman was that most people would not have to personal fortitude to be their own god. The fact that Nietzsche failed in the end may not in and of itself recommend that all men would, but his case illustrates that most people do need a construct of meaning larger just than themselves. Modern western social architects have simply failed to provide a replacement for those that worked in the past.

Confucianism is an example of a belief system that successfully indoctrinated society with non-nihilistic meaningfulness using non-religious premise centered in social responsibility rather than in typical fear / reward philosophies inherent in most religions. Over time, Confucianism was infected with religious pollution, but initially its anti-nihilistic success was only secular.

All in all, I don't think we can point to secularization alone as the cause for increased susceptibility to nihilistic tendency in modern societies. It is just that many of the most influential modern intellectuals have not understood what it is that gives a society deep cohesive meaningfulness. There are many candidates for meaningfulness that could work here, not only religious options. For example, Auguste Compte used "Humanity Itself" as a focal point for a positivist religion with some success. Whatever the focal point might be, modern social engineers have largely marginalized that factor in their systems of philosophy and education.

SOME COMMENTARY ON THE KOREAN DIET

There is the old traditional Korean diet which consists of mostly vegetables that have been treated with powerful flavoring techniques. These techniques include a desiccating phase (*either by drying or salt treatment)*, and a re-moisturizing phase where very deliberate and specific flavors are forced back into the vegetable matter by absorption. They do this to leaves, stalks, roots, and other plant masses that would be inedible without this kind of processing. I believe Koreans could make wood chips and cardboard taste good.

Older Korean people eat mostly traditional foods; rice, different types of Kimchee, special Korean soups, and small side dishes of specially flavored veggies, fish, pork or chicken. Fruit is often desert. Korean traditional soups have very rich broth, fortified with bean pastes, and hot pepper pastes. Soy sauce and sesame oil is huge too, for flavoring otherwise boring fish and veggies. It is all quite delicious and healthy.

Korean Women's Food

Korean women have a list of herbs that they feel are beneficial specifically for women. Suk, or mugwort, is one such herb, and women make something called Sukduk (chewy Korean rice cake) with mugwort. Many older Korean women still go out into the mountains and find mountain herbs. They call it NAMU, which is kind of a catch all word for all green growing things. There is a list of NAMU that is reputed to be specifically good for women. These ideas are relics of the Chinese medical tradition that is still highly respected here. Pomegranate is another fruit that has a reputation for being good for women.

Public Food – Cheap, Clean and Healthy

At home or in a Korean company or government office, traditional type foods like described above are often the predominant category. A lot of companies have cafeterias with lunch for 2,000 or 3,000 won. Many Government buildings have these cafeterias too, and people just eat their mid day meals there because it is cheap, convenient, healthy and tasty. Besides, the the Korean work schedule doesn't allow time for anything else. Outsiders are welcome to eat at most of these cafeterias, and if a person ate their main meal of the day there, their monthly food bill would go way down, and that person would be a lot healthier for it. Many universities have the same kind of open arrangement.

Junk Food Generation

But younger people seem to be loading up on a lot more processed Western style junk food. When I go to the market here, and I see inside other people's carts, it scares me the amount of garbage people are buying. In the past ten years, the items at the grocery store have really proliferated in these kinds of pre-prepared, unhealthy food categories. And many homes also have cabinets stocked with junk food that the family snacks on (*although regular meals are still traditional, often with simple rice, kimchee, and Korean soups*).

Two Worlds of Food

So I would say that there are two worlds of food here. One is traditional Korean, and the other Western processed foods. The older generation sticks mostly to the traditional, and the younger generation mixes both worlds freely these days. With the exception of some specialty NAMU, there probably isn't much difference between what Korean men and women choose to eat.

Most Healthy Diet in the World

Korean food is touted to be one of the most healthy diets on the planet, and I agree generally with that, at least in principle. But the regulatory oversight in the food sector is not that good. Restaurants are sometimes dirty. A lot of the vegetables are coming in from China too. Some feel this might be one of the reasons that Cancer in Korea has been on the rise.

HOW HAS KOREA RISEN IN OLYMPICS PERFORMANCE OVER TIME?

As an expat American living in Gangneung City, South Korea, of course I am interested in Olympics History here. Gangneung is the sister city to PyeongChang, and many of the 2018 winter Olympics events will be held here.

A Little Bit of History

Koreans have been participating in the Olympic games since the 1930s, during the time when Japan dominated Korea. But the 1948 Olympics were the first contests where she competed as a sovereign nation.

Korea's performance record at the Olympics didn't really start to shine, however, until the 1980s when Korea began to win gold. Since then, the number of gold medals that the nation brings home from the games has been on the rise. What is it that accounts for this change?

Admitting to my shameless indulgence in rank speculation, I suspect there is more than one answer to that question. Allow me to explain.

Internationalizing Korea's Population

First of all, The 80s and 90s were times when Koreans in general started to become more interested in the outside world. Prior to that time (as we have mentioned before), travel outside of Korea was severely restricted.

Internationalizing Korea's Economy

Then, in the 1990s the IMF crisis led to more foreign investment in Korea, and this in turn to more international ties. As the general population, the commercial sector, and the government became more internationally concerned, is it a coincidence that the nation began to do more at the international games?

Another factor may simply lay in having a more healthy, more wealthy society in general. Many Koreans born in the 60s and 70s are smaller in stature and appear more 'life worn' than people born a decade later. There is certainly more opportunity to focus on the arts, academics, and sports now than there was in the past. Perhaps having an increasing pool of healthy candidates from which to draw also resulted in higher quality Olympic teams as time went on.

Whatever the reason, Korea began bringing home more medals from the 1980s until now. And the trend still seems to still be upwards. It will be interesting to see if it continues during the current cycle of games in Rio and in PyeungChang.

WHAT IS THE BEST CASE TOWARD NORTH KOREAN DENUCLEARIZATION?

Regime change is one route to denuclearization. If that happens, there are two likely scenarios. Either a puppet government will be set up under the guidance of the USA and South Korea, or the reunification will proceed.

Regime change is not such a far-fetched notion. Although brutally repressive governments have been able to hold on to power for long periods of time, things are changing regarding information control, not only in North Korea, but all over the world. The rise of an informed people with the means to communicate and plan is a scenario that could very easily lead to populace uprising and toppling of the regime.

Agencies in the South have been supporting clandestine programs of info-proliferation in the North, and North Koreans are now becoming mobile enabled with phone adoption. The units are only NK enabled out of the box, but a black market exists where international sim cards can be purchased and switched out.

SK also has a pretty large NK defector population, and they do both radio and TV programming that is broadcast into NK and smuggled in on USB drives.

Another path to denuclearization would be normalization of the existing regime. This seems unlikely, but it is not impossible. Convincing the young leader to join the community of nations might not be that difficult considering that he has murdered all the old hardliners, and could kill anyone else who dissents. But one wonders about the war crimes aspect of the scenario.

For one thing, it would be hard to swallow the injustice of accepting his regime considering the horrible humanitarian record. Secondly, he seems likely to have sold his soul to the devil per say, and might be past the point of any reason, which seems the likely situation.

Toppling the government from within seems the best scenario considering the threat that an open campaign would pose to Seoul as well as the resistance that would be put up both by Russia and China. A military solution is not really supported by the SK government or its people either.

DO KOREAN PEOPLE NEED WALKING LESSONS?

I was looking at a forum the other day, and an interesting questions was raised. "Do Korean People Need to Take Walking Lessons?" Although the issue was raised in a rather disrespectful manner, it does point to an interesting perception that Westerners have regarding Korean walking practices. The issue could relate to the way many Korean people use roadways and sidewalks, and how some Korean people do what my wife and I call "heel walking" in the apartment above you when you are trying to sleep. My parents would not have waited for the downstairs neighbors to complain before they taught us to walk on the balls of our feet instead of our heels.

It is a knee jerk reflex sometimes, to try to define all anomalous behavior in cultural terms. And there may be some cultural factors involved in Korean walking practices. For example, it seems that many Asian cultures do not fear traffic as much as we have been taught to do in the West. I regularly see Korean people waiting for the walk light, standing not on the sidewalk, but out in the road way with the cars passing so close to them that the wind messes up their hair. It is even worse in China. It looks like some kind of bravado sometimes. But I don't think it really is.

The reason I say that is because I also see parents who grab the hand of their little kids and dash out into oncoming traffic, dragging the little ones behind them. This not only passes that disrespect for danger on to the next generation, but it also counter evidence against the bravado theory.

Another interesting behavior is when the older Korean guys, with their hands clasped behind their backs in the typical Korean dignity pose, actually walk deliberately out in the road way, almost like they are challenging your instinct to beep the horn at them. They seem to believe that due to their age, they can impose inconvenience on strangers who would be breaking some Confucian code of honor and respect to dare honk at them or warn them that their display is unwise

But there are many roads in Korea that are old style, and which don't have any sidewalks, or even painted lines. It is still a kind of free for all on these roads. So I wonder if people have a hard time making distinctions between the those and the modern streets with sidewalks and crosswalks. I find that when I am walking with Korean friends, although there is a huge modern sidewalk right there, I am often the only one using it. Usually, the Koreans will walk along right out in the roadway without really even thinking about it.

As far as 'heel walking', parking out in the middle of the road, cutting in front of you in line, elevator etiquette, hawking up giant lugers and spitting big oysters on the street, and many other behaviors of this type, I don't really think there is a cultural angle on that. I mean, all cultures have families who educate their kids in basic niceties of social etiquette, and families who don't. We just call it basic home training, and there are families here who have it, and ones that don't. This is the same in any community you visit. It is a matter of putting the comfort and welfare of others ahead of, or even at par with your own. That is really the basis of good manners, and it is not a natural trait. It must be taught and learned.

My wife says that Korean people can tell if you had an education right away by how you act and talk. I think the same is true anywhere. The civil rights movement and the attendant unrest associated with it initiated Lyndon Johnson's investigation into the racial / economic /educational divide, and it is not just in America that we see that all three follow the same basic fault line. Minus the racial aspect, it is just as true in Korea as it is anywhere on Earth.

DRIVING IN KOREA – ORIENTATION FOR NEWBIES

Driving in Korea is an important topic, and one that is close to my heart. I was able to get my license here quite easily, but you do need a valid drivers license from a country that Korea approves in order for the ease to translate to you. USA, Canada, Germany, UK, etc.. are all countries that Korea recognizes. If you don't have a valid (*that means currently NOT expired*) license, then you have to go through the entire written and driving test. Alternatively, you can get an international drivers license from your home country before you come here, and then drive with it for a year before it runs out and you have to do something more complicated.

Initial Adjustments

In my first couple years of driving, it was a constant frustration and stress for me. People here don't seem to look before they step out into the street, and I was constantly fearful of killing someone accidentally. In many ways, the driving habits are really different from somewhere like the US or Canada. Rules are not really rules here as much as they are suggestions, and the police don't interact very much with drivers. One of the worst things for me was when people break the obvious rules of right away.

That Might Not be Rude

Korean drivers also do a lot more of what we in the US would consider rude, inconsiderate driving here, although I don't think Koreans necessarily see it that way. When that happens a lot, my tendency at first was to drive more aggressively, but that was not smart. I had to adjust. There are too many factors here that demand caution and defensive driving, so aggression on the road, in any form, opens one up for fender benders. Let me explain some of the factors I am talking about.

Set Backs – NOT

In the US, it is illegal to park or build close to the corner of an intersection because of the visibility issues. You can't block the view around corners. In Korea though, many times you have to pull out into the oncoming lane in order to see, and even then, you can't see far because of people parking right on the corners. It is really risky so you have to be defensive about it.

A Stack of Bricks

Spaces are small. Parking is difficult. And to make it worse, somehow Korean people believe that turning on their flashers and parking right in the middle of the road is a better idea than walking 500 steps from a parking place that is really not so far away. Honestly, when I first moved here I secretly fondled the idea of keeping a stack of bricks behind the passenger's seat to huck through widows of these inconsiderate and selfish parking criminals. But I have gotten used to it now after 8 years and have become a bit more tolerant and understanding in my heart about it.

Politely Being Impolite

When people don't stop at intersections, we call it a California Stop in America, and you get a good ticket if you do it. But when people do, they do it quick so as to avoid interrupting the flow of traffic. Here, however, people very often do California stops, but instead of doing it quick, they somehow think it is better to go slowly. It is really interesting. They will even bow to you and wave as they do it.

The Korean Stare

Finally, there is the Korean Traffic Stare. If you make a mistake, or even look like you are going to, an old Korean driver will usually just stop in the middle of everything, forcing other drivers to stop too. Then he will sit there and stare at you disapprovingly while everyone waits for him to express this strange traffic ritual. If you bow to him apologetically, he will still hold your gaze for a minute before he moves on, but if you don't acknowledge him, he will sit there longer.

For all these reasons, aggressive driving is a bad idea. But it will take some time for you to get used to the different modes, attitudes and ways. Like anything else, differences can rub you the wrong way at first, but if you stay at it, you will get use to it and be just fine.

IS KOREA CONTROLED BY AMERICA?

To suggest such a thing would likely be fighting words to most Korean people, who are fiercely patriotic due to the strong military stance that has been maintained here over the last half century. All Korean men between the age of maybe 23 and 36 have to spend a minimum of 2.5 years in the military service.

Along with that, there is a powerful sense of history here due to the amazing record of Korean kings of the past. The court recorders for the Korean kings wrote down pretty much everything they did on a day by day, hour by hour basis, and an added aspect of uniqueness to this was the fact that the Kings and their families were not allowed to read their histories during their own lifetimes in order to protect the ability of the recorders to be frank and truthful in their writings.

Korea people therefore, related powerfully to their national and cultural identity in ways that most people can't really understand. But there is another interesting aspect of Korean culture that makes them really passionate about their uniqueness and autonomy. It is the poetic tradition.

Educated Korean people from past centuries were rated on their ability to speak in extemporaneous poetic prose. That tradition can still be seen in the melodrama of their movies and dramas and in the poetic entertainment where emotion just floods the room until your socks are soaked with it. That passionate tradition transmutes to their patriotism almost without loss. You can hear it in their popular songs, and I think it greatly contributes to their love of drunken Karaoke indulgences.

After the Korean war, the USA chose a few family dynasties to use in economic partnership, and America also backed up a semi-puppet government that allowed US control in some more or less limited ways, depending on the category of US interest. The Korean nation and people have really benefitted from favored status from the west since then, and this can't be denied. It also can not be denied that the fortitude of the Korean people and their tenacity, their work ethic, and their conservative values have contributed amazingly to the rise of the nation and the retention of their autonomy as it has re-shaped itself to fit the modern world. Does the US still control Korea? Did they ever?

It seems fair to say that a stronger argument for US control could be made the closer we get in time to the Korean war, but that those controls have morphed into cooperation as more and more times has passed.

IS SOUTH KOREA A DEVELOPED COUNTRY?

Absolutely, yes. In certain ways, Korea could even be called "ultra modern". Living in a typical American home is like living in a cave compared even to some of the more average apartments here. But there are some interesting qualifiers to that overarching, predominantly positive response.

Korea is an interesting mix of developed and non-developed. It is a contrast how you can see an ultra modern high rise apartment right beside a traditional mud house with small logs for rafters sticking out from under corrugated roofing sheets from the 1950s. Right in the middle of the busy modern areas, people will plant these little gardens in any strip of available dirt. You see elderly Korean people pulling rickshaw type recycling wagons along behind them walking down the side of a modern 6 lane highway.

Physical Development Outpaces Attitude Development

The buildings look developed from a distance, but when you get up close, you see that there is a lot of details that aren't up to the standards of countries like US, Canada, or Europe. It is hard to find a truly square corner anywhere. The infrastructure under things is often slapped together in a hurry up kind of manner, cutting corners and creating problems down the road. You can tell by the stench that rises up from under all the cities. This happens in many countries where surface development outpaces the development of quaint, ignorant, or lackadaisical agrarian type attitudes that need to be upgraded to successfully match and underlie the upgrades in physical development.

Looking Poor but Being Wealthy

Regarding poverty, of course there is some. But don't let the pity pictures fool you. Some of these street vendors, beggars, and garbage collectors have saved a ton of cash over the course of the decades, and are not poor by US standards. Many of them have sacrificed everything to put their kids through college, and they live their lives frugally but comfortably in an old world way. Some really are poor, but most only look that way. In many 'developed' countries, it is the other way around. People look wealthy but are really poor. Here, some people look poor, but are actually quite stable.

Culture Aspects – Do They Fit The Modern World?

Korean culture has been changing to adapt to a modern world, but the basis of the social structure is not "developed". They still follow a strict authoritarian exclusionist iso-cultural pattern that was imposed on the spirit of the region a thousand years ago to protect it from adaptation and change. It is ultra conservative and although it is comfortable on the surface due to the friendliness and hospitality of informal relations, it is also harsh and painful for people from other cultures to try and work together with Korean management or governmental systems. They are so closed minded and Confucian in their world view, and it is almost impossible to get them to realize that the 500 year old Korean way is not the only way, indeed not the best way in a modern, globally integrated world.

ATTACKED OR IGNORED – I CHOOSE KOREAN STYLE

Living in a culture that is radically different from my own, there is often the need for 'difference bridging' efforts. It could be around a matter that I don't understand, or on something that I disagree, but either way, there are sometimes points of friction that require a combination of communication, meditation and time in order to reconcile. On occasion, reconciliation is not really root level. It is only adjustment perspective on top of the values that I developed in formative years.

Movement Toward Unreasonableness

At the same time, I recognize in my own culture a movement toward unreasonableness, and I suspect this is rather a global thing. Take a look at politics, for example, and the breaking up of communities into smaller and smaller fighting groups. With the advent of social media, we are able to get our thoughts out in the open more fluently, and there is an inherent risk to that these days. There seems to be a lot of haters out there who have pretty closed minds.

Being Ignored

In Korea, it sometimes irks me, because a lot of the times when I don't understand a Korean person (*usually an older guy*), their accessibility for communication is pretty much nil. They just avoid the subject completely. But at least they don't launch into unreasoning tirades. It is hard to say if they are reasonable or not because they simply won't share sometimes. They might be hiding a very valid perspective inside their heads, but they just won't communicate it outwardly so there is no way to tell.

Of course, in America where I grew up, my parents taught me that respectful communication was the way to bridge differences. Silence doesn't really do it, and neither do tirades. I think there is more to that perspective than just culture. There seems to be inherent truth in it.

Being Attacked

On the other hand, a lot of times communication breaks down when there are differences between Westerners. We call it ad hominem fallacious reasoning, where people simply attack you as a person instead of calmly pointing to any factual disagreement that they have with your viewpoint. It happens a lot more now than I ever remember it happening before.

So, whether it is Korean style of unreasoning where a person simply refuses to engage, or Western unreasoning where someone engages, but in an unreasoning way, it seems that sharing your thoughts these days is sometimes less successful than you may have hoped. Fortunately, there are people who are reasonable in every culture, just as there are people who are not.

But when there are disagreements with Korean people who will communicate, there seems in my experience to be a higher occurrence of respectability and humanity in the exchange that leads to understanding, not to frustration. Overall, I'll have to go with Korean people on this one. I think there are more of them that are easier to deal with in that way. I'd rather be ignored than attacked, I guess. But even better, I'd rather talk about it instead.

IS THERE A EUROPEAN EQUIVALENT TO YANGBAN?

This is a good question. Remembering that Korean culture has received much influence from China, it seems that the Mandarin tradition of educated 'aristocrat' might be a good match for the idea of Yanbgban, although the use of the word aristocrat comparative to the Asian bureaucrats is not a clean match.

Asian Traditional Education Credentials

Where-as in Europe and in many other countries, the elite in society came into their positions through inheritance, the educated Mandarin class in China received their status through education. Rich and poor alike could rise to the pseudo ruling class of civil technicians, and they could not pass this status on to their children. Education was the ONLY way to attain the position. Noting like this came into existence in Europe, I believe, until the French. Henri de Saint-Simon and people like Auguste Compte began the elevation of educated operatives in Europe, although along somewhat different lines.

Saint-Simonian Technocrats

Henri de Saint-Simon believed that if all the princes, aristocrats, and priests died, society would continue on without really noticing, but if the engineers and technicians died, civilization would pretty much end. The European concept of the technocrat was born in that era, and Napoleon the 3rd took up the idea in his 1830s empire. Saint-Simonian technocrats (*as they were later called*) held civil and bureaucratic posts in his Napoleonic regime.

The Philosopher Should Pull the Stings

In my mind, Yangban and Mandarin share more in common with French Technocrats than with the aristocratic or royalist traditions of other European management systems. They all followed in the tradition of Plato and Confucius, who both believed that the philosopher should pull the stings. Although Mandarin and Yangbon were educated mostly in tradition, and not in science, and although technocrats were rooted in scientific training rather than in custom and tradition, education was the one thing that brings all of them into commonality, not only with my thinking, but with the general recommendation of both Plato and Confucius.

HOW DO YOU EVALUATE KOREAN WOMEN?

Korean people in general are amazing in many ways. Korean women are the most devoted and self sacrificing mothers in the world. And yet, the picture of the average female here is a generationally changing one, as it is in pretty much all cultures these days. Let's talk about three generations then, grandmothers, middle aged women, and younger women. In all cases, there is a noticeable difference in the way educated women behave as compared to less educated people.

Korean grandmothers are intensely loyal to family as a rule, and have been willing to show amazing patience toward mistreatment by a sometimes chauvinistic society. They would endure a lot of harsh treatment by their husband and his family and still never give up on their marriage. But a lot of times, the older they get, the more power they have in the family. While the husband retires and his life becomes smaller, the wife comes into her own. Usually, their patience pays off and they get relief from the harshness in the end.

Middle aged Korean women used to take a lot of abuse from their husbands and their in-laws, but few will tolerate it anymore. Their children are the most important things to them, even overpowering their relationship with their husbands. More and more, middle aged women are not averse to dumping their husbands if they feel things are not working out, and there are a ton of women now in the professional work force, where-as that never used to be the case with the older grandmother generation. And Korean women are some of the most hard working people I have ever seen, often putting the men to shame in my mind.

The young generation are have what we call the princess syndrome in Korea. Their parents have often pampered them and shielded them from any responsibility all the way through childhood and into their adult life so that they are in no way either inclined nor prepared for life in the real world. Considering the history here for wives, it is understandable that fewer and fewer women are opting for marriage, and there are a lot of single ladies around who refuse to give up their freedom for the drudgery of married life. For this reason, a lot of men in the countryside are looking to foreign wives from Cambodia, Philippines, and Thailand for marriage partners.

The beauty industry has created a problem for young and middle aged women too. There is so much competition over surface looks that there may be some shallowness there in the younger generation. You can sense the jealousy, rivalry, and contention.

All of the above is just my impression overall, and is a portrait painted in sweeping generalities. And I in no way mean to suggest that all old Korean men are overly harsh to their wives, or that all in-laws oppress their daughter-in-laws. I have seen a lot of families that are amazingly dignified and high level in their interpersonal behavior.

All this having been said, I still suspect that there is something in the above that will make pretty much everyone angry, so let me apologize in advance. It is a pretty hard question to approach.

WHAT REALLY IS CULTURAL DIVERSITY?

I think of cultural diversity similar to the way we think of genetic diversity. When a group from a large family splits off from the main population and moves away, becoming isolated by mountains or oceans, and when no interbreeding occurs, the two groups will begin to develop traits that are unique, each to its own local family, tribe or nation. The longer the split endures, the more distinct the differences can become. Isolation over long periods is the catalyst for genetic diversity.

In the same way, when a group is isolated and keeps to itself for extended periods, they develop different ways of viewing and responding to matters. In areas that were peacefully undisturbed by conquest for longer periods, the more difference there is in culture as compared to other groups.

The idea that cultures can retain their autonomy in a multi-culture world is rather a misnomer, I suspect. They can try, but become swiftly bastardized and blended. Keeping the surface, visible aspects of a culture in glass display cases is mostly what occurs, but when the grandmas and grandpas start to pass on, the younger generations retain less and less of what a culture really truly is on the inside. Cultural diversity is an isolationist phenom, and mixing it up is anathema to cultural diversity, any way you cut it.

COMPARING WESTERN AND KOREAN CHILD DEVELOPMENT PATTERNS

When I first moved to Korea, I was a bit shocked at the leniency by which Korean parents guide their children. Compared to my parents and other families I know, there is a stark difference in the gentleness and sensitivity that Korean parents show to their children at a young age.

On the other hand, it is actually sad, even depressing to see the pressures that come onto Korean kids starting with Middle School and on into High School. Does it balance out? How does this pattern compare to how I grew up? Are there patterns that by comparison bring insight to both sides?

In a previous article about the Korean generation gap, a member of our editorial staff commented on this difference, and he was right. Parental controls seem more tight on younger Western kids and tend to relax when we get a little older. And in some ways, this appears opposite the situation here in Korea as described above.

My Childhood Upbringing

I can portray a bit how my parents raised me a half century ago. In doing that, I have to admit some changes have occurred in American parenting patterns too. As an old guy, I predictably don't approve of all of them.

My mom and dad were totally on the same page. Us kids (*my sister and I*) knew absolutely where the boundaries were, and there was swift and irrevocable retribution for crossing, even coming close to them. My dad always explained things to me. He would take long, extended effort to reason with me and make me understand. Then he would say, "So, I'll have to spank you if you mess this up." That seldom happened though, because he would always give me a couple chances to mess up before the hammer fell. The result was that I always knew I deserved it whenever it happened.

My mom was a bit different. She was loving to us, but had a backhand like a striking cobra. There was no talk with her. She knew that we knew, so why talk? That was her philosophy.

Little Discipline – Little Respect and Appreciation

I have had private students here in Gangneung whose parents are that involved in teaching their young ones to be polite and very high level. But I don't know of any Korean parents who have ever used corporal punishment like mine did. More the rule of thumb here, at least in my experience, is parents who let their young ones get away with 'murder'. They often treat their parents with what to me appears to be high levels of disrespect and a dependent kind of entitlement attitude. Again, not all are like that, but a larger percentage.

However, I know in my heart that Korean family and Korean society is more demure, dignified, tame, and respectable than American. Somehow, without a lot of strict training in the formative years, Korean kids come out of it pretty peaceful and conformist, fitting rather nicely, if not always comfortably, into their tightly defined roles.

Macro Discipline on Societal Level

The primary factor in Korean society that I attribute this too, admitting limited insight, is the responsibility that society takes up in providing a pre-set, ubiquitous structure for the kids and the parents to all fit into. One thing that people complain about in the West is that schools don't teach any ethics, and often neither do parents. When parents do teach ethics to their kids, it is a mix match of different religious and philosophical ideologies that can never fit with the multi-patchwork of a 'melting-pot' background. In that environment, even with a strict upbringing, there is a lot of contradiction inherent in a young person's world view, and the parent's viewpoints too.

In Korea, that is different. The schools take up the subject of ethics, and their approach matches with all of the parent's ideas too, as well as with the grandparents and all the neighbors. It's funny how, even where I think Korean ethics are upside down, I respect them for the agreement. There is a powerful positive to that universality.

It all Makes Sense – It all Evens Out

In a society like this, parents can afford to be less watchful and less intense about helping their kids fit into society. Society makes them fit in more automatically. Parents may even feel like protecting their kids a little from that, knowing that in Middle School, conformity will start, and that loss of freedom is something everyone knows must take place. Secretly, they even seem to rue it with at least half of their hearts.

Please excuse me if I'm wrong in these matters. These are just impressions from spending 8 years, and three or more hours per week each in about 50 homes over the course of that time. I have had some students from early elementary until high school, watching them, even helping them grow up. You really grow to love them, and their parents too. It really is a beautiful society in many ways. But it is also very different.

TEN THINGS TO ADJUST LIVING IN KOREA

There is a pretty steady population of Western foreigners living in Korea, but a larger portion are transient. When teaching contracts run out, new teachers run in to fill the voids. If you want to fit in and maybe avoid some friction, consider the following list of ten:

1. Korean Drinking Culture.

Yes, Koreans drink together to make friends and learn about each other. There are certain rules for posture, and for not allowing anyone's cup to be empty. Also, never pour for yourself. Wait for a minute, and someone will refill for you.

2. The Semi Celebrity Status

There are areas in Korea where most people have still never spoken to anyone other than another Korean. They will stare at you, wave at you, and approach you like you are some kind of famous person. It is getting better as time goes on, but you still find it happening on occasion, even in Seoul.

3. Overcome Karaoke Inhibitions

Korean people love "NoraeBangs" (Singing Rooms). They get drunk and sing these overly emotional, melodramatic Korean songs. It doesn't matter if your are a good singer or not. You should join into this shame-fest if you want to fit in. Just get a couple of drinks on standby to condition yourself before it is your turn.

4. The Korean Picture Pose

Don't think just standing there with a smile is good enough when you take a picture with your Korean friends. There are two choices in a good Korean pose. You can do the 'Old Guy' pose, where you can't smile at all or your dignity will be crushed. The other option is the 'Goofy Pose' where you make a 'V' sign, or a heart with your fingers. There are other variations to the goofy pose, but don't try one that hasn't been proofed by Koreans first.

5. Dinner for Breakfast

Korean people don't really distinguish food types for different meals. In the US, breakfast is definitely in a category all by itself. Lunch and dinner are more interchangeable, but there are still pretty distinct lunch food traits and dinner food traits. In Korea, you can just get the left-overs from last night and eat them in the morning. It's pretty disconcerting at first.

6. Collectivism

People don't really do much that is meaningful as independent agents here. You have to get your social connections on board if you want to do anything important. Since you won't have a social group when you first come here, you will have a hard time doing anything really substantive. It is best to stick to the limited roles that are assigned for you until you get a lot of friends. Independent agents seem to threaten Koreans and make the withdraw.

7. Kibun

Kibun is the idea of maintaining an even mood, politeness, and consideration. We Westerners can be emotionally expressive, and that's ok, but as soon as we express intense emotion, Korean people will lose respect for us. We have to bite our tongues and smile on the outside a lot. It can be hard until you get used to it.

8. PpalliPpalli Culture

PpalliPpalli means hurry up and do it even if you haven't really thought it through that well. If you screw it up because you hurry, that's ok because you can just hurry up and fix it.

9. Nunchi

Nunchi is the ability to read between the lines. Chicks love this, but it's hard for guys to get it right. You are supposed to be a good enough listener to understand a lot of what hasn't been said. You do this by reading body language, facial expression, and winks and nods. The only problem is that you can't wink and nod. It is nice in a way, but sometimes frank communication is needed. Korean people usually won't tell you stuff straight out.

10. Tit for Tat

If a Korean person does something nice, they usually expect you to reciprocate in kind. If they take you out for lunch, they will pay. They don't do dutch well. But if they pay for you one time, they really expect you to do that for them sometime soon in return. If you are Korean and you don't reciprocate, you'll be in the doghouse. There is some leeway in this for foreigners, but you can't change the basic negative impression of being and inappreciative slob if you don't show return kindness.

Of course there are a thousand other little things that are different in Korea, but that's what makes it such a pleasant place to visit. You will most likely enjoy it for a year or two, if you are even a moderately tolerant and mellow personality type. If you stay longer, you will have to deal with some of the deeper discomforts. But don't worry about that now if you are new. Just enjoy Korea. It is a beautiful country, culture and people.

WHAT DO YOU THINK ABOUT FOREIGNERS WEARING HABOK?

I am an American married to Korean, and when we were married (23 years ago) my wife brought a huge Hanbok (I am 6ft 7inches) for me to wear at our engagement party. The Korean tailor thought she made a mistake when she ordered it and gave him the size.

My wife's sisters came to the US with her and stayed about a month until our wedding. It was important for them to have the engagement party, and I went ahead and wore the Hanbok. Just so you know, the color for men at engagement is hot pink, so that was a big challenge to my machismo, but I sucked it up and went along with it. But my face was just as pink as my suit. Hopefully that gained me their eternal respect - lol.

I tend to agree with Jayson Wayne's sentiments, although perhaps women have more of a fashion nostalgia for hanbok, and even for me, I find a female foreigner wearing one is less strange that a man. But when I see foreign men (westerners) wearing hanbok it just seems a bit pretentious and out of place, except maybe in a formal or family situation like I described above, where they are wearing it because they are expected to do so, and you kind of know they are squirming a little inside it. But to each his own, and I wouldn't judge. It's just my impression and I'm in my 50s, so I might be a codger about it.

But for Koreans, the reaction may be different. Korean people are intensely proud of their culture and they think everyone else will be interested in it to the same degree that they are. For those of us that have been around the world a little, most old traditional cultures have unique clothing, dances, instruments, etc... that are mildly entertaining but sometimes outright silly. I think Korea's traditional dress is more dignified that some others.

I know it isn't exactly politically correct to say this, but I would probably more readily wear a Hanbok than a Kilt, for example. And those guys don't even wear underwear traditionally. And think of those Japanese shoes that squash your feet until they are tiny, or the Ubangi lip and ear inserts that make your lips bigger than a dinner plate. Like I always say, just because you can doesn't mean you should…

WHY DO KOREAN PARENTS STRESS THEIR KIDS SO MUCH?

It is true that Korean kids are stressed academically. Parents are often overbearingly strict and demanding about school. What is it in Korean culture that accounts for this? I think there are quite a few factors that go into it.

Government Influence

Korea is a small peninsula with little in the way of natural resources. The government has traditionally told the population that the only resource they have is the intelligence and educability of the people. This ties in directly to the strong Confucian background, where education is the most important factor in creating the refined human.

High School Centered Pressure

The school systems are set up quite differently here too. In the West, middle school and high school is an increasingly intense experience until you reach the apex of academic demand, which is college. But in Korea, university is actually much less demanding than high school. The problem is, if you don't have a good high school record, there is no way you can get into a decent college here. This situation places more stress on the younger demographic, often with sad results.

Form Over Function

Korean culture is what I call 'form over function'. What that means is that it matters less what you can do, and it matters more what paper credentials you have collected. Kids keep a portfolio of all the extra awards and certificates they have acquired all the way up from kindergarten through their entire adult life. The more papers you have, the better case you can make for being meaningful in the world, even if you can't find your way out of a closet by yourself.

Overscheduled

I have students whose days are scheduled out every hour from the time they wake up, until the time they pass out. They have regular school, then they go to two or three Academies. Then they have a private tutor, or even two, who come to their homes for personal classes.

Hyper-Competitive

Korea is also one of the most competitive environments I have ever seen. Even little siblings compete mercilessly with each other. Not all are like that, of course. But parents who have been infected with the competition virus also infect their kids with it. And like I said, although it is not ubiquitous, it is very common.

Crowd Mentality

Sometimes I reason with my student's parents, arguing that science proves over tired, over stressed kids actually under-perform rested, balanced kids. They admit it, and they know it, but they still insanely pressure their kids. When I ask them why, they say that they have to because everyone else does it too.

There are a few reasons for the strange phenomenon. I guess time will change it, but until then, Korea ranks near the top for stress related student suicide.

CREATIVITY IN KOREAN STUDENTS

In the old days, when I first moved to Korea, my overwhelming impression was that Korean kids had a problem with creativity. That impression was a blanket kind of reductionist viewpoint, and I picked it up for good reason, but lately, after being here for 8 years now, I am re-evaluating that impression again.

Indoctrination Into The Social System

First of all, there is a pattern to a Korean youth's indoctrination into the social system. At a young age, there is little expectation placed on them and they are relatively free, as all children are pretty much all over the world. They are very creative at the elementary school stage, and intellectually courageous, willing to take risks and to make mistakes.

Pre-Formed Education and Activity Experience

This having been said, the activities and the educative methods that the adults bring to the kids are patternistic at best. Rather than creating a lot of imaginative art in art class, for example, they do paint by numbers sort of projects. Instead of playing music that they try to make up, they only play music that other people have composed. There are many more pre-formed educational and activity based experiences that adults press in on kids, so I think that begins to dampen down and inhibit creativity a bit at those early ages. But that may not be the really big thing.

Individuality Inhibition

As time goes on and the kids get into Middle School, the social expectations begin to weigh more heavily on them. Asking questions in class is not encouraged. Being an active learner is frowned upon. Memorization and recital of information is more important than interacting and understanding. And the pace, volume, and intensity of the learning experience is somewhat crushing. This creates a certain environment, atmosphere, and mood that is not conducive to individuality, and individuality is necessary for personal creativity to flourish.

A Bubble of Freedom

With my private students, I can create a little bubble of freedom from all that. I am not Korean, so when the kids are with me for the three or 5 hours per week, they can get completely out from under those societal expectations. In that setting, even Middle School and High School student's imaginations come back alive, full of brightness, sparkling eyed and excited.

So, I have to conclude that I have not been witnessing the kid's lack of creativity at all, but it is the social structure that throws a wet blanket over their individuality and the spontaneity required for joyful creativity to blossom and sprout.

I'm not here to judge Korean society. I find a lot that is different, a lot that is positive, and a lot that is uncomfortable in it, but no place is perfect. I love Korea. I just can't help feeling a bit of pity for my students, and for most Korean kids; especially once you have spent enough time with them that they get a little stuck in your heart.

ARE THERE ANY GOOD THINGS ABOUT NORTH KOREA?

That is going to be a hard answer for pretty much anyone to tackle since very few people go in or out, and individuals who go in are not allowed to see NK as it really is. But I can answer on principle that there must be some good things there. Here is what I mean.

East Germans who experienced both the communist era and the democratic equivalent were nostalgic about the old ways, because they didn't have to worry about money, doctors, dentists, education, or whatever. This doesn't mean that they had good alternatives compared to the west, but just that they didn't have to worry about it.

People in agrarian countries are jealous of more advanced countries, but are sometimes generally happier and less stressed out. I heard of a lady in South America who had a strange condition where she always had twins or triplets whenever she got pregnant, and by the time she was 60 years old she had more kids than her age. You could never do that in developed land. The cost would be outrageous.

I am not saying that having 60 kids would make anyone happy, nor living in an undeveloped country, or in a repressive land. What I am saying is that perhaps there are unlooked-for positives in any situation, but they may not be laying there on top and easy to discern.

I suspect that there are a lot of NK families in the countryside who live relatively peaceful lives in an old world way. The food issues a decade ago must have disrupted that for sure, and even now the govt is pretty invasive, taking all the food they can get from the farms, but it wouldn't be too hard to shuck away enough and hide it from the collectors so that you could survive without stress, and in the rural areas, I am sure a lot of people manage to do that.

An agrarian existence is one where you work half days and half years, and you spend a lot of time sitting around scratching your butt. Many in the west could use a little more butt scratching time and a little less stress.

IEK MEETS THE MAYOR

Today, the Mayor of Gangneung City was kind enough to meet for lunch with IEK executives. Gangneung is the sister city of the PyeongChang Olympics, and officials here have a growing interest in foreign visitation. The purpose of the meeting was to discuss Olympics Preparedness and how visiting foreigners might feel when they come here in 2018. Along with the Mayor, four other members of the Gangneung Olympics organizing staff joined to express some positivity toward iExperienceKorea. They encouraged our desire to be of some assistance to local Korean service providers as we get closer to the time of the big events.

The Mayor's Kind Concerns

The Mayor spoke at length about his real concern that visiting foreigners should have the most positive experience possible when they come. This reflects the real and sincere hospitality that Korean people honestly feel. He told about how Korea has made big changes in the general view toward foreigners from the 1970s and 1980s. Now, there is quite a positive basic view from Koreans toward Westerners, and that is good.

iExperienceKorea's Desire to Help

As far as iExperienceKorea is concerned, we told the Mayor our belief. Gangneug residents are warm, friendly, and hospitable enough that Olympics visitors are sure to have a positive time here when they arrive. The one thing we suggested was that if the Korean providers were are comfortable with foreigners, the foreigners will be more comfortable in Gangneung too. It just follows. Our suggestion was that we try to facilitate more quality interaction between Korean service providers and Western foreigners in general. That is what iExperienceKorea is all about.

An Exciting Hope for Western Foreigners

The most practical aspect of the meeting was when IEK spoke about our experience riding in the Taxi to patronize local restaurants. We described our impressions of actually trying to engage the taxi and restaurant personnel at a higher level of foreigner interaction. We explained how we would like to help bring more foreigners into Gangneung as time goes on leading up to the Olympics. That is when the Mayor offered the idea of sponsoring some type of 'not yet defined' foreigner events.

A Lot of People Could Help Out

Nothing has clearly materialized as of now, but our hope is that the city will act on that good idea. Not only would 'foreigner events' be good for Olympics preparedness, they would be good for visiting Western tourists too. According to recent census data, there are around 135,000 Americans living in Korea now. Probably about 100k are US military personnel. There are 25,000 Canadians, and around 7,500 from the UK. This is a really large body of foreigners (close to 170k) within a few hours from Gangneug. The potential for increased local multicultural exposure is high, especially if there is some special incentive encouraging foreigners to come.

Let's hope that the local governments in both Gangneung and PyeongChang take action on the Mayor's good idea. It would be great to increase expat traffic to this beautiful area on the Eastern shores of Korea.

KOREAN TORTURE AND SLAVE CAMPS IN THE 1980S

Back in 1988, Korea hosted the Olympic games, and it was widely considered to be a success. Nations are eager to hold the games because it provides them with economic stimulus, and also a chance to project a positive image to the world community. But Korea has a skeleton in the closet regarding it's Olympics preparedness effort back then. It is a horror story that the government is still trying to cover up. The refusal to take responsibility for the abuse and murder of socially disadvantaged in the 1980s is a specter that haunts the reputation of the current Government of Korea, and hosting the games again in 2018 brings that problem into the spotlight, even against efforts by the current government to perpetuate the cover-up.

1980s Olympics Preparedness – Crime Against Humanity

In the 1980s, Korea was still under a dictatorial government, and part of their Olympics preparedness strategy was to clean up the streets of Korea. What this clean up amounted to was rounding up anyone who looked a bit disheveled and rushing them off to state supported concentration camps where slave labor, sexual abuse, and deprivation ended the lives of many innocent victims. Many of them were children who are still alive, scared with the memory of the experience.

Current Korean Dishonor in Still Covering it Up

Thousands of survivors are alive in communities across Korea, and the vast majority of them remain silent due to the strict Confucian system that still weighs heavily on their perceptions of their relationship to the community at large. To this day, no one in the government has been held responsible. In the private sector, which actually ran these camps ostensibly as programs for social responsibility, no judicial retribution has come down either.

Protecting Her Father's Legacy?

It was Park, Chung -he, the assassinated dictator and father of current president, Park Geun-hye, who gave the directive to start cleaning up the streets in 1975. The police and local community members worked together to identify undesirables and truck them off to a life (or death) of slave labor in a growing constellation of camps which expanded to about 36 nationwide. By the mid 1980s there were more than 16,000 people detained. Child rape was rampant, and murder systematic.

A young Busan prosecutor finally lead a raid on the 'Brothers' facility in 1987, and the owner, Park, In-kun was found to have about $5 million in currency from embezzling government support funds and from slave produced products sold abroad. It is interesting that there were Protestant religious supporters of these Korean humanitarian atrocities just as there were Catholic supporters of Hitler and the Nazis in the 1930s.

Underlying Issues When Politics Eclipses Justice

Clearly, modern Korea 30 some years later won't have this kind of atrocity going on. But a recent story about Police raping High School girls was swept under the table just as the scandal of the Brothers camp is still being ignored and denied. In social life too, the injustices that are perpetrated on the lower ranks in society are ignored and denied because the perpetrators have the power, and there is no one to defend the oppressed from the oppressors. As a foreigner here, I have experienced this on a small scale in Korea myself.

I recognize the positives of having a strict, military style, authoritarian hierarchy over society. Part of the reason I love Korea is due to the peace and predictability that comes through this Confucian preset. But we have to admit the ironic truth that our strength is sometimes our weakness at the same time. Being honest and sorry is the first primary step to being forgiven, and that becomes easier when representatives are a generation removed from the crime.

But some horrible criminals who are still alive today maybe should not be forgiven. The fact that they are still in power does not protect them from humanitarian guilt at this level of atrocity. And there is the real precept of guilt by association. A sitting president who is a family member of a culprit, and complicit in currently covering-up and protecting living criminals surely demands some kind of attention in a matter as grave as this.

WHY IS THE WESTERN WORLD SO SUCCESSFUL?

I assume that your idea of success is in the descriptive, scientific way that we have been able to comprehend nature and bend her secrets to our will, creating weapons and consumer goods, putting men on the moon, and curing diseases like childbed fever and smallpox (though some say we created AIDS when we did).

Another aspect of success might be in mass education, raising billions of people out of illiteracy and ignorance and preparing them for a productive life in an industrial and information tech world (though some call this a modern form of slavery).

Yet another definitive of success could be the tolerance and human rights standards that were set at the turn of the 18th century and that the west has fought for over the past 200 years.

Some people would argue that pre-modern societies are actually more successful than the west in other ways, but lets not go into that since it doesn't seem within the scope of this question.

The light of scientific and social advancement could never have burst forth in a repressive, overly authoritarian and ultra conservative, mono-culture society, so the reformation against repressive Catholicism in Europe was important, as well as the patchwork of different peoples and languages present there.

There was a lot of blood spilled in intermixations that all reacted upon each other in that European micro-sphere, all leading ultimately to some type of more tolerant democratic, or representative rule. Tolerance is required for progress to occur. Ultra-conservative right wing constricture, (like that of the catholic dark ages) or unrestrained opulence and grossly irresponsible rule (like the aristocratic Machiavellian courts of the day), simply chokes out innovation and motivation, effectively squelching the progressive forces required for advancement in knowledge along with social change. These constrictive influences simply had to be overcome, and it was very expensive to do so.

China and most of the Asian cultures retained their backward facing posture (and left to their own still would) while European religious and aristocratic calcification broke up and parts of Europe were able to turn around in places like England, Holland (and America), and finally in France as well, as soon as the Enlightenment influence was able to shirk off the straight jacket of the Catholic dragonades and the vestiges of the inquisition that still remained until the French Revolution.

Max Weber pointed to the powerful motivational factors involved in Protestantism in the book, "Capitalism and the Protestant Work Ethic". In the book, Weber argues that the idea of frugality and responsible resource husbandry became evidences that a person was one of the pre-destined select where-as laziness and poverty was evidence that an individual was pre-destined to burn in hell. He claims that this was a huge impetus to the adoption of capitalism and an investment mentality among protestant believers, and that where Catholics pushed Protestants out, like in Spain, the power of that work ethic and progress it engendered was strictly retarded and authoritarianism continued to stifle both progress and the free mix of peoples and ideas.

Greek, politics, thought and language was a huge factor too in western progress too, most notably in the democratic ideal along with the teachings of Aristotle. Importantly, early church fathers were able to meld some of Aristotle's thought with the Judeo-Christian philos thus preserving and promoting Aristotle's uniquely scientific approach to natural classification methodology, metaphysics, ethics and logic. Copernicus, Galileo, and Newton, along with Francis Bacon really cut their teeth on Aristotle, as did John Stewart Mill, whose book on Inductive Reasoning is still required reading for experimental scientists today.

Germany's contribution, which was huge in the field of chemistry and philosophy, was largely motivated by a sheer disgust from and intolerance after decades of French revolutionists and Napoleonic Imperialism sticking it's butt in the German face. Hegelian notions of individual National Exceptionalism really spurred German intellectuals to a fever of progressive activity which boosted the west higher up the scientific ladder. But European progress was already pretty well along by that time.

Language is important too, and the Latin languages are uniquely rich in both vocabulary and syntax, beside being quite easy to learn as opposed say to Chinese. Some say that it took 20 years of study for Chinese scholars to attain sufficient literacy, and by then they were so old and traditionalized that a sort of inevitable conservatism naturally created a conceptual permafrost that stymied progressive thought. This is just one example why a good language is necessary for rapid progress to ensue.

America was a place unencumbered by aristocratic impediment, and empowered by her distance from the debilitating wars of Europe. While the old world was decimated by religious wars in the 16th thru 18th centuries, next the revolutionary and Imperial wars in the 19th century, and then the world wars in the 20th century, America mostly stayed out of it all on the Monroe Doctrine, benefited from Europe's insanity, enriched herself, and blew the top of any inhibiting restraint on social and scientific progressive advancement, subsequently projecting that advancement out in all directions to all nations and peoples open to it.

KOREAN BULLYING IS A DIFFERENT ANIMAL

Bullying is a form of injustice where someone in a position of power or authority behaves unfairly toward someone in a lower or weaker position. In a militaristic, authoritarian social setting, this will happen, but I don't think of it only as bullying, which is quite a general term. When bullying happens within a structured authority system, it can become a much more specific thing.

A Hierarchical System of Authority

Of course simple bullying happens in Korea, where it is not part of a cultural system of authority. But I see it all the time coming from older Koreans toward younger ones, from bosses toward their employees, from politicians toward their underlings, and the list goes on. There is a hierarchy here, and when hierarchical operatives are just in the expression of their authority, it can be a genteel system, and that was Confucius' intention when he crafted the philosophy behind his optimal society. But noble authority figures turn out to be the exception, not the norm, and the bad examples trickle down, manifesting in general behavior among the populace.

Language Bullying

There is even a from of language bullying that Koreans use against each other as they vie for higher ranking in their social pecking order. For example, they will use respect words (*honorifics*) toward each other in some cases, and then revert to disrespect words in other cases, changing their approach where they think they can score points of social politics.

Establishing Rank Amid Uncertainty

The goal in this behavior is to establish rank in social situations where there is uncertainty. What I mean is this. When a bunch of Korean people enter a room, there is an immediate, unconscious recognition of who is above you and who is below you. But then there are those who are at your same social level. It is among these of similar rank that competition occurs to establish some order in the flux. This is bullying among equals and is a bit different from bullying from above. But both happen systematically in this society, and it is sometimes pretty ugly.

The Attitude Underlying a Systemic Bully Culture

I was going to ask a Korean friend to help with some computer programming one time, and his older Uncle told me not to ask, but to bully him into helping me. His reasoning was that I was older than my friend, and demanding service from him was the appropriate thing to do in this society. I'm not citing this necessarily as a case of bullying, because there are different ways that it could be viewed. But it points to an underlying attitude that can lead to a lot of unfairness being perpetrated upon the younger ones, and on ones in positions of lesser 'authority'.

The Solution Can't Come From the Problem

One of the standard ways of dealing with bullying is to approach someone in a position of authority and to report it. That would mean talking to a teacher or a supervisor, depending on your situation. Unfortunately, in Korea you likely won't get a lot of help that way. It can work in America where there is no strictly codified authoritarian paradigm. But when the problem comes from the authority structure, the solution won't likely come from the self same source. The most common response to this kind of report in Korea may well be political and will take the form of a cover up together with ostracism toward the one seeking help. It is in the interest of people to choose sides not based on what is right or wrong, but based on political factors, like who has most power, or which side might deliver the most social benefit.

Resignation Equals Emotional Control

One thing that a bully tries to do is to destabilize their victim emotionally so as to take advantage of that. They try to put you in a weakened position so that it is easier to disrespect you and to get others to do the same. The best answer to that is to stay in control of your own emotions. You can do that by watching how other Koreans do it. They accept their rank and position with resignation, and they shut up and suffer in silence. This society is full of suffering people who are being crushed under the weight of unfair authority figures. Me too. And there is usually nothing that can be done.

If you are a foreigner like me, your best option is to stay on the fringes of society until you get pretty old. There are sectors, like in the education industry, where Korean society has created these little bubbles of relative comfort for us where nothing much is expected and they understand not to burden us with their style of social expectation and pressure.

If you can't avoid interacting with the political side of Korean society at work or at school, you are going to have to eat a lot of crap to survive. So you may need to get a lifetime supply of toothpaste. But here are a few tips that might help if you have the fortitude to apply them.

THE FIRST KOREAN WAR – 1871

Back in the 1800s, America was vying for trading space in the far East, trying to compete with Britain, Portugal, and the Dutch. The colonial powers were still at a high point, but the exploits of France, first with the revolution and then with Napoleon's disruptions, had taken a lot of wind out of Europe's sails. England was firmly taking the lead on the world scene, and America had established herself as a rising contender. But she needed trading partners that were yet unclaimed. Korea was there, undisturbed, and waiting to be courted into someone's harem.

There was a problem however. Korea was uninterested in outside associations. Following the isolationist principles of cultural purity that inundate Confucian protectionism, Korea rejected American overtures with a strong hand.

A Firm Rejection

The first effort by America was advanced in the 1840s, but it was simply ineffectual, so the idea was shelved for a few decades until 1866. Then, a brave American captain and crew attempted to approach Pyeongang to establish trade, and to talk religion. Of course American sentiments at the time were strongly Protestant, and the missionaries on board did not stop to consider that maybe the Koreans would not distinguish them from the Catholics that they had knowingly been prone to execute. But the Koreans soon made themselves clear.

The ship, called 'General Sherman' was repeatedly warned off by the Koreans, but the captain, with a mixture of bravado and stupidity, ignored the warning. The Koreans were serious however, and they attacked the ship, setting it ablaze, and killing everyone on board.

Finding Out What Happened

Of course, the American government had no news regarding the fate of that ship. About a year later, in 1868, another American ship was dispatched to investigate. They learned a few things on that voyage, which was ostensibly a treaty mission.

First, of course, they learned that the Koreans were disinterested in any treaty with the West. Secondly, they learned the fate of the General Sherman, which was like an emphasis point on the NO!

US Retribution and a Change of Mind

So a few years later America sent a military expedition to Korea in 1871. They succeeded in taking an island outpost and engaged successfully with the more primitive Korean forces. The record says that around 350 Koreans were killed while the Americans lost only 3 men. But the cost of a full scale invasion of the mainland was deemed not worth the return. Korea was a pre-modern society then with little to offer in the way of ROI. The Americans withdrew and left Korea to its agrarianism and its seclusion.

But around the year 1878, Japan forced Korea to open it's previously isolationist policy, and in 1881 Korea finally did sign an insincere treaty with the USA. The differences between East and West were stark however, and the lands were discouragingly geographically distant. Korea and Japan continued to interlude on quite a personal, if not jovial basis, but America was still a long time in coming to relevance here.

It is interesting to note that the effort was made however, and that a tiny war, long forgotten, was waged between the two countries about 150 years ago.

WHY IS THE LEFT IN AMERICA SO OBSESSED WITH THE ISSUE OF CULTURAL APPROPRIATION?

The answer to this question might trace back to Karl Manheim and his sociology of knowledge theory and Ludwig Wittgenstein later, with his different forms of life. The premise that bound both of them together was the idea of relativity on a socialistic basis.

Manheim talked about a society as the custodian of a body of knowledge that no single person in the society could ever hope to assimilate in total. But members of the same society would have a shared and unique over arching perspective on the world that differed significantly from other societies, because each society's particular body of knowledge would always be arranged differently.

Wittgenstein took that idea further, saying that when two cultures differed, a member of one culture could not adequately critique the ideas of another culture from the outside. It would be like one guy playing soccer, and the other playing basket ball, and there would be no mesh between the two, so the soccer guy couldn't tell the basketball guy that he was wrong in any meaningful way, and visa versa with the basketball guy toward the soccer guy. The only thing you could say was "This game is played." It would require one to learn the other's game in order to participate or critique in a non-destructive way.

Epistemic relativism is the down-stream result, to where not only normative matters like culture and ethics are relativistic, but also even things like the weather and scientific fact could be true in one culture but false in another. We might want to say, couldn't you test and see which view produces better outcomes, and then maybe one could prove to the losing culture that your way is better? Ludwig Wittgenstein point, as well as Manheim, was that you couldn't do that from the outside, and even to try would be a cultural offense doing more harm than good.

All the derivative flavors and complications that now attend cultural diversity can be traced straight back to Manheim and Wittgenstein. And while I don't have a horse in the race, frankly I have issues with epistemic relativism as an ideological outcome, and think the cultural sensitivity sometimes goes to far if it isn't reactionary toward some injustice. What I mean is that there is really no need for knee jerk cultural sensitivity where no harm or insult is meant. In prejudicial or bigotry situations, it is entirely another story though. And there is a lot of that still in the world.

A BOY AND HIS SNAILS – GANGNEUNG STORY

There is an apartment complex in Gangneung called "Hillstate", and it is maybe one of the most desirable neighborhoods in the city. A really nice 8 year old kid named Sungjun lives here (*Korean age is cardinal, not ordinal, so it is one year older than Western age system*). He has snails for pets.

Snails Aren't Cuddly

When I first heard of snails for pets, I thought it sounded quite novel, but after seeing them grow, and seeing Sungjun care for them, now it seems like a great option for kids to have these kinds of creatures as pets.

Actually, maybe the idea of a pet doesn't really apply too well. It is more like a science project, or a zoology thing. I mean, the thought of a pet usually carries connotations of cuddly little creatures that give you some kind of emotional payoff. I don't think snuggling up to a snail, or even to a fish, is a very appealing thought.

A Good Option for Apartment Pets

The point is that when people live in these clustered apartment situations, they are often pretty secluded from natural things. This is kind of a handicap when it comes to development of appreciation for nature and living things. It is hard to have a dog in an apartment, because everyone gets mad at you about the noise. Cats are a better option, but having a cat cooped up in your apartment with you can drive both you and the cat crazy.

I think fish are a good option for an apartment 'pet'. But one thing I learned from Sungjun is that snails are cool too, even though I am not quite ready to try one myself.

KINDNESS OVERCOMES DIFFERENCES – GANGNEUNG STORY

I had the rewarding privilege of spending my Chusuk vacation days staying on a small farm in a rural area, helping and elderly Korean couple upgrade some of the facilities in their home. In doing so, I spent many hours with a Korean Halabogee (Grandfather). As I did the construction work, he supported me, and we learned a lot about each other, even without many words. His English is zero, and my Korean is about 2.

Two Problems in the Farm

One of their problems is exposure to the weather, because one side of their house was completely un-insulated. We built an insulated wall with two doors to provide protection this winter, and added some storage space in the process.

Another problem was people invading their space. Sometimes criminals or drunks would just walk up to their house, steal from them, or simply start banging on the door late at night. Needless to say, the lady of the house felt quite vulnerable and insecure. So we built a locking gate system to prevent that kind of easy access to their home

The Erosion of Time – Social and Material

The gentleman of the house is an old aristocrat, who never really had a job in his entire life. His father left him quite wealthy in land holdings, and early in their life, they had servants, nannies, maids, and quite a privileged life. Some 45 years ago, village construction crews build for them what was then the nicest house in the area. Over time though, construction standards have improved while their house has deteriorated.

Another type of deterioration was palpable to me on this trip as well. Of course there is the change of status in society when one ages, and here that comes with an interesting irony where people become both more respectable and at the same time in some ways less.

But maybe the most subtle drift over time parallels somewhat a similar, though much older trend in the west. I am referring to the loss in status of the aristocrat in Korean society.

Policy Strains Landowners

It is difficult to sell land in Korea. The government has some complicated rules about it, and at the same time, they started taxing land quite heavily. This situation places this gentle couple under a burden at times. That's why we spent 4 days there helping them out. They offered us money at the end, but we refused, accepting friendship as the richest reward for our effort.

Dignity Without Politics or Pride

I have had many good experiences with Korean men because of the dignity and quite spirit that they often learn culturally from an early age. But that nobility is sometimes polluted with the intense social politics of a hierarchical systems that rubs me the wrong way. I think I have expressed that here on this blog numerous times. But on this project, I was able to experience the pure good of that aspect of Korea, with none of the negatives attached. The beauty of it served to change and sooth me.

Living in Gangneung is great, but it gets a bit claustrophobic culturally at times, and there are limitations to ones capabilities due to language and cultural barriers. The quiet, contented life of this Korean grandfather, his patience, kindness, and humility, served to remind me that being meaningful or relevant need not be an externally projected thing. With him, he achieves personal poise and balance by staying true to what he believes are core principles of goodness, and all of them are internal unto himself and how he defines himself as an individual person.

Dropping the 'Now' Perspective

I live my life quite disconnected from the patterns of nature and the rhythms of seasons. My perspective is clouded by 'the now' in that my connection to any ancient heritage that grounds me is abstract at best. This kind Korean Halabogee that I spent this valuable time with is not so concerned with 'now'. He has a historical, cultural, traditional grounding that is tempered even more by his agrarian life. He farms his land himself, helped by neighbors whom he helps in return, and is not disrupted by much of anything outside of himself or the boundaries of his sphere.

I found in this vacation season, that zeroing in on what you love about a culture and people can really help to balance out what is uncomfortable and displeasing about it. Truly, there are extremely beautiful aspects to this culture and people.

HOW DO SOUTH KOREAN MEN FEEL ABOUT DARK SKINNED WOMEN?

Interestingly, Korean people are still rather prejudice when it comes to dark skin. It is not just a beauty industry phenomenon, but something that runs even within their own people. Koreans with dark skin have a status maybe less impressive among them than Korean people with lighter skin.

As for most Korean men and their taste in women, light skinned Korean women would be by far the most preferable in terms of both physical and behavioral attraction. When a Korean man does go outside his own culture for a partner, it is usually within the Asian races that he would first look. The darker the skin, the less easily integratable a spouse would be into the Korean family and culture.

As with most general answers however, there are a lot of exceptions to the rule, and it would be prejudicial for me to attribute blanket prejudice to an entire nation of individuals.

PARSIMONY AND MAGNANIMITY – A KOREAN CONSERVATIVE EVALUATION

Prominent in English Literary History is the work "Leviathan" by Thomas Hobbes. In it, he laid out an interesting balance comparative between being timid and over reluctant, and being risky and spontaneous. It is certainly easy to see the need for individuals to be able to balance the two sides in order to make the wisest, most effective decisions. But different cultures are prone to different tolerances and reflexes in the matter.

Liberal VS Conservative Risk Tolerance

Obviously, liberal progressives are more prone to make experimental changes and take leaps of faith into new, uncharted territory, while conservative traditionalists are more likely seek historical confirmation for their positions and commitment decisions. Korea is traditional and certainly reflects the conservative trend. Korean people take almost no risk on untried or unproven options, and the Korean demand for specific formal credentials is nearly unbendable.

Failure Is a Kind of Learning

This tendency often brings tension to westerners who live here. Part of the Western tolerance for what is new comes from the tradition of inventive creativity, trial and error development, and the confidence we have gained over the past 200 years of inventive success in the West. We are not so afraid of failure. In fact, we definitely view failure as part of a development process that we recognize and clearly define.

Yet while it is true that failure can lead to success, there is a cost to it, and the successes only come to those willing and able enough to follow through no matter what those costs turn out to be.

When You Have to Take Risks

In Korea, creativity and exploration are discouraged at fundamental levels, and what appears to be parsimony as Hobbes would have defined it, sometimes results. Probably in disaster situations, this recalcitrance is most damaging. Circumstances where there is no time to test outcomes for that kind of secuKrity are sometimes forced upon us, where doing nothing is just not an option.

My father was a missile tech on a nuclear submarine, and his skipper pounded it into the heads of his sailors that sometimes even doing the wrong things was important, because at least you would be directed by that toward something that you could do in situations where doing nothing would lead to certain death. Fortunately, it is not always, maybe not most often, that parsimony proves disastrous.

Failure is Expensive and Valuable

Without trying to be critical of anyone, it is interesting to compare differences. And I will definitely agree with the Korean point of view that doing the new thing is expensive and risky, where-as letting others go first is often the safest choice, at least for you if not for them.

I guess I have become more conservative too, as I age. This is maybe natural. But looking back at my exuberant youth, many of my historical mistakes and failures are the memories that are the most valuable to me even today. They still serve me well in that when I do decide to take a magnanimous risk, they are always there to guide me.

KOREAN CULTURAL IDENTITY – CONNECTING THE INSIDE TO THE OUTSIDE

Most traditional cultures have affectations that are more meaningful to themselves than to outsiders. Native Americans, for example, beat drums, dance around fires, and smoke peace pipes. While it is fun to watch them with their feathered head dress, painted faces, and tasseled buckskin breaches, the deeper meaning of this behavior is often lost on us as we lightheartedly leave an exposure to a Native American cultural show and quickly move our thoughts to the newest movie or our favorite pop song.

To the Indians, however, these ritual behaviors have deep meaning which personally relates them in real ways to everyday aspects of their lives, relationships to each other, and to the world around them. Putting on a show is easy to do as an entertainment function, but to communicate the relevant cultural meaning of it is entirely another challenge. How can a culture connect the inside meaningfulness to the outside showiness?

This question seems important for Korean Olympics organizers, because one of the overt goals involved in holding the games is to communicate to the outside world 'Korean Culture', and yet, have we really clearly defined what that even means? Are we talking about the outside things, like the traditional dress, the sideways double drums, the swirling headed hat dance, or the eerie wailing music that seems to haunt the soul when you close your eyes and really listen to it? Or are we talking about the family values and humanitarian sensitivity, the dignity and respect, the safety and peace of the society?

The importance of these questions to Korean people might not seems so high because for them, they can see the intricate connections between the behavioral, visceral, tangible culture performances and the more subtle, meaningful aspects of the culture that makes it truly beautiful in a more enduring, human relatable way. It seems that the inside qualities of the society are what will attract outsiders in a much more powerful way, although the performances are fun, entertaining and interesting in their short term, touristy fashion.

The challenge for anyone serious about making the outside connect with the inside might simply be in defining something like this: How do the Korean drums (Buk) relate somehow historically to the security and safety that is so restful in this society? A clear focused message answering a question like that would certainly make travelers want to experience the culture. Or, how does the dignity and respect in this society connect in some way to the ancient style of Korean dress? All visitors wish to be respected by their hosts, so highlighting a connection like that at a cultural performance might really drive home the benefits of coming here for a vacation experience.

Communicating these kinds of connections seems important, but not the first step for those who design the cultural projections that visitors will experience when they come here. The first priority would be to define the connections. Then communicating them should be quite a simple and pleasant matter.

For most people, the dancing, the singing, the simple musical instruments are a fun novelty, because all old traditional cultures have similar rituals, and they all seem to blend together for travelers into a montage of pleasant color, motion and sound. From South America, Africa, Europe, Alaska, etc..., so many cultures have these ancient rituals that we enjoy watching and clapping along with. But what is it that really differentiates one from the other? What is it that makes them all start feeling kind of the same? What is it that will make a Korean cultural experience any more powerful, memorable, attractive, or enduring than any of a hundred others?

Hopefully the thoughts in this article can help answer those questions, not only for organizers, but also for tourists in the destination decision process. For local planners, it would be a great success if more tourists decided to come to Korea rather than settling on some other option.

WHY DON'T WE SEE MORE SIMILARITIES BETWEEN CULTURES?

I think we do see more similarities than difference, but we tend to focus on the differences more than on what is the same. There are some obvious reasons for that, as follows.

One factor involves friction and discomfort and could be illustrated by our awareness of our own bodies. We usually don't focus on our toes for example, unless they are uncomfortable. Pain causes us to pay attention to them. Otherwise the fade into the background in our prioritization of what requires attention. It can be likened to that one student who causes trouble in a class. It is usually that kid that rather unfairly gets the lion's share of the attention.

In personal relationship the same thing often happens, where someone does 10 things that are nice and good, but one thing that is unkind or unjust, and it is our tendency to forget all the good stuff and focus in on the bad. Why? Again, because it hurts us in some way and pain is pretty demanding of our attention, tending to shut out all else, at least for some episode of intensity, but then we just remember the intensity, which compounds the relationship problem with another layer.

Another factor, however, is perhaps a bit more sinister and systemically contrived. It hinges on the fact that if a group can be differentiated from all others, it becomes a power base for the leaders. Look at large professional associations for example. Maybe the vegetable growers of America becomes a powerful lobby. So within it there develops the Corn Growers of America, the Beat Growers, and so on... But within the Corn Growers of America, the Sweet Corn guys and the Indian Corn guys decide they want to carve out their own power base, so instead of emphasizing their commonalities, they purposefully emphasize their differences in order to hack out a new population of associates over which and from which they can gain and wield authority and power.

This is exactly what culture wars are intended to do from a 'national engineering' standpoint. And while culture differences are legitimate and sometimes thorny to bridge, nation builders have found them to be a convenient crux upon which to turn masses of people against one another and foment differences that demarcate us away from each other so they can ride heard on their fiefdom, YOU AND ME!!! This is exactly why we have over 230 different nations now, all fighting about our specific individual cultures, not willing to bend toward a brotherhood of man, but always focused on diversity, which is just a softer word for divisiveness.

I respect other people's cultures, and actually enjoy the difference for the most part. But my father would spank me whenever I allowed my own self importance to jeopardize kindness ore reasonableness to the point that it lead me to become the perpetrator of selfish injustice and pig headedness toward others. The leaders of our nations don't have a dad to spank them though, and the slobbering masses are simply too brainwashed and nationalistically indoctrinated by now to recognize what is really going on.

HOW DO YOU UNDERSTAND THE RELATIVE SAFETY OF ASIAN MEGACITIES? WHY?

There may be some factors that contribute to safety in large Asian cities. The more punitive the law, and the more active the police, the less crime there will be at large, obviously. I think China and Singapore may have stricter statutes, but for sure, conservative Asian countries have more legal strictures than we do in liberal progressive lands. And we tend to protect individual rights rather to an extreme that you won't find in the east as a rule.

Another factor is going to be poverty, because when people are desperate there will be higher risk of crime. Poverty is not a problem so much in Singapore, Japan, and Korea, but it is still huge in China. However, in the cities poverty is less of an issue although Chinese rural areas still suffer badly from it. In smaller Chinese cities like Dalian, we experienced tourist predators about 10 years ago, but I don't know if it is better now or not. I am speaking mostly to the "why" here since my experience is mostly in Korea. And since China is such a huge place, different jurisdictions seem to have different standards and situations regarding crime.

A third factor might be social cohesion and the collectivist mindset you often find in Asian lands. That has to be an effective crime inhibitor in general, and we see the collective mentality in all 4 countries mentioned above. People are more concerned about their reputation and that of their family here, and the social restraint is has a positive effect to discourage potential bad actors.

In his book "The Sacred Canopy", Peter Berger pointed to the Nomos (a neologism referencing a society's world view) as a limiter on behavior. If a society has a strong nomos, the indoctrinated masses will be more psychologically unable to break the codes of the culture. He used the example of a European man well indoctrinated in Christianity who fantasized non-the-less about group sex with a harem of some sort. He proposed that even if a such a man with a well set nomos found himself in a situation where he could act out his fantasy, his nomos would make him impotent and it wouldn't work out for him in the end. He would simply be physically unable to perform.

I don't know how much stock to put in Berger's analysis, but I suspect there is some truth to it, and by that measure, the collectivist nomos of eastern cultures should act as a preventative influence regarding anti-social behavior, and I think it does.

In Korea there is crime, but compared to the west it is so limited that I almost don't notice it. We have run into scammer activities a couple of times over the internet or the telephone, although they are quiet easy to recognize. I have never felt in danger here or worried about being on the streets in the middle of the night.

EAST / WEST – BARRIERS TO COOPERATION

For many months western foreigners have shown interest in assisting local organizers to help prepare service and hospitality providers to welcome the throngs that will descend on the culturally myopic east coast of Korea in just about a year and a half from now.

How This All Got Started

The story of this effort started for some of us about six months ago when representatives of Gangneung City approached us in a series of meetings where 5 City employees rather high up in the Olympics administration here explicitly asked us for help. The results since then have been interestingly dismal.

Six of us got busy right away. We crafted suggested programs for preparedness in multiple areas of need and approached different departments at City hall. We also ran some powerful programs ourselves to demonstrate that we had the ability to perform in critical ways that are needed. The response from all departments at all levels has been always the same: 'We can't work with you because of our internal politics.'

The Politics of It Leave Us Out

To put some insight into that 'politics' statement, Korean operatives are under the direction of their department heads. Foreigners have access to the operatives, but not to the heads. So the operators can't work us into programs without the approval of the department oversight, which has already approved ongoing programs that don't include foreigner input. Seemingly, these programs can't be adjusted at this point. Why? Because of politics. But we can't really go over the operators and approach the bosses directly without creating friction among everyone. So here we sit on the outside.

Multi-Culture Experience Deficit

An intersting blind spot that the Korean organizers have relates to the fact that they have no multicultural experience, nor do they have language training experience. The western foreigners here obviously have both, but the city has failed to make any room for us to meaningfully help. One sad result is that the programs they craft are less effective than they could be.

Some interesting differences in the way Korean people see things compared to westerners can be observed in a couple of simple scenarios. In

(1) language training we could make some observations, and we could add some insight perhaps in (2) gaining westerner's support for preparedness programs as well.

Language Training Problems

On the point of language training, the City seems to be operating on the premise that they will get the local providers comfortable enough with English within a year and a half so as to be able to have adequate exchanges with visitors at the games. We don't see that as a realistic goal however. In the taxi, restaurant, and hospitality sectors we are talking about mature people with busy lives. And even if it were possible to get thousands of people onto some kind of English program for three hours per week (because that is what it would take), one and a half years would still simply not be enough time to help enough people to make any real difference. Not to mention how cost prohibitive it would be to do so.

To us, a better approach would be to create a tool like we have on iExpereinceKorea.com and to have auxiliary material built up on that where users could practice and improve the use of target phrases in their service sector. We already did that as part of our initial preparation when the City asked us to help.

On our site, one web page for each service sector has both the Korean to English, as well as the English to Korean phrases. The phrases are hardcoded, simple, and essential to functional communication in the taxi sector, restaurant sector, and hospitality sector. And some small brochures are prepared for more practice if the providers want to learn more. But they wouldn't have to because the tool itself is so self explanatory and easy to use.

We have experimented with Genie Talk, which is a suggested app for translation at the games. Although the application is cool, and it does work, it is a bit quirky and sometimes takes multiple tries before it actually functions. It may take eight or ten exposure interludes before providers started feeling comfortable enough to use it. With a hard coded solution, it might only take one or two exposures. This is just a report from our own experience using both.

Getting Westerners to Spend Time with Korean Providers

Gaining westerner support for preparedness programs is a delicate subject as well. We usually don't like to join things, and we need to be brought on board in the right way. Korean people respond very differently, and it is apparent that organizers here don't actually understand these difference subtleties. For example, in the supermarkets here, they often have amplifiers and microphones with a vendor yelling about the apples, or the fish that are on sale. Korean people seem to flock to those loud events, but westerners are likely to have just the opposite reaction. We are not easy joiners, and we don't like to be yelled at or to stand in line with a crowd.

Another example is the attendant shopping mentality that Korean people have. It seems they view an attendant's presence as a sign of courtesy during the browsing phase of a shopping episode. Westerners by contrast, might see that hovering attendant as intrusive and pushy.

There are a myriad of other little differences like the examples mentioned above, and pointing at them here is not to say one way is better than another, but only to point out that there are real differences. If preparedness program organizers have no awareness of these factors, how will their efforts ever gain any broad foreigner support?

Korean Wet Blankets

At IEK, we have tried to point out some of these factors, but it is hard to talk about them. We are often blamed as being negative, or as complaining. This response just emphasizes the problem of multi-cultural engagement with a mono-culture majority. To date there has just been little openness to work with on the mono-culture side. Frankly, our initial enthusiasm for helping has experienced the dampening effect of many Korean wet blankets to date. And it hasn't really helped to remind officials that they asked us for help. We didn't ask them.

ABOUT THE AUTHOR

Jeff Rogers has an educational background in Medicine, Science, Journalism and Philosophy. He has been a businessman all of his life, and now has been living in Korea with his wife for more than 8 years.